About tl

Jacqueline, a recently retired nurse, was born in England in 1960, to Irish Catholic parents. As a child, she aspired to work in a hospital, and started training as a Registered General Nurse in 1979. Following her qualification, she trained as a midwife and completed a Diploma in Person Centred Counselling.

She worked mainly in women's health, and spent many years teaching medical and nursing staff, as a University Lecturer and an Associate Trainer in Primary Care, with a clear goal of encouraging health care workers to increase their awareness and skills around communicating with sensitivity and kindness towards those in their care.

Jacqueline is passionate about empowering women to develop the self-awareness and the confidence required to be their true selves. This passion has developed over time as a result of her own journey towards self-realisation and a drive to share openly the lessons learned from her personal experiences.

Acknowledgements

Dedicated to:

My amazing husband – who has lovingly encouraged and supported me every step of the way during the long gestation and birth of this memoir.

My son and daughter, who really are the best thing that ever happened to me.

Ravi, and the baby, who helped me to learn by cracking my heart wide open.

Special thanks to:

Paul Bowes for his editorial oversight, and to Ann Bowes for inspiring me to be brave enough to put my stories onto the page and out into the world.

Tracey and Steve Moren at Moren Associates Limited for the design of the book and cover.

Becky McMurray for her beautiful painting for the front cover.

Sally Siddons for facilitating the printing of the book.

My very patient friends and family who have listened to me telling my stories, read my early attempts at writing, and supported me in the darkest of times. There are too many to list – but you know who you are!

The Oasis and the Butterfly

A Memoir

by Jacqueline Farrell

"There is no such thing as a problem without a gift for you in its hands.

We all seek problems because we need their gifts."

Richard Bach (from Illusions – The Adventures of a Reluctant Messiah)

The Oasis and The Butterfly published by Book Castle Publishing, June 2022

ISBN: 978-1-906632-17-5

Printed in Great Britain by TJ Books Ltd

Editorial material and arrangement © Jacqueline Farrell 2022

Cover artwork © Becky McMurray 2022

The moral right of the author has been asserted

Contact the author:
email: farrelljacqueline704@gmail.com

Book bibliography:

Illusions – The Adventures of a Reluctant Messiah' by Richard Bach
1977/8 Pan (ISBN 9780330253550) 1998 Arrow new edn (ISBN 9780099427865)

'The Tao of Physics' by Fritjof Capra
1975/6 Fontana (ISBN 9780006341024) 1992 Flamingo new edn (ISBN 9780006544890) 2010 Shambhala special edn (ISBN 9781590308356)

'Feel The Fear and Do It Anyway' by Susan Jeffers
2012 Penguin Random House UK (ISBN 9780091907075)

'Women Who Love Too Much' by Robin Norwood
1984/5 Arrow (ISBN 99780099482307) 2004 Arrow new edn (ISBN 9780099474128)

Music references:

'Lean On Me' by Bill Withers 1972 Sussex label
'Bright Side of The Road' by Van Morrison 1979 Warner Bros. label
'Desperado' by Eagles 1973 Asylum label
'The Deep' by Lucinda Drayton 2003 'Bliss' album Blissful Records label

Author's note;
The name of every person in this book has been changed, apart from my own, to protect confidentiality while maintaining relevant facts.

Contents

Preface

This is a true story. It traces my quest to understand how my life experiences have shaped me as a person. In writing this book, I have sought to find meaning in my responses to many traumatic events, always searching for the gifts which problems will inherently bring to us. One such gift taught me how being a 'people-pleaser' can sometimes ultimately cause great harm to oneself. I have paid a high price for it in so many ways.

Memory is always subjective. Other people in my life may of course remember things from a different perspective. It is impossible to recall conversations verbatim after so many years have passed, but some of the dialogue was so traumatic at the time that it will be forever etched upon my memory.

For my mother

1

Behind a Painted Smile

(The Isley Brothers 1969)

As I walked the one-mile journey into work, I kept my fist tightly clenched around the small pot of semen in my coat pocket, trying to keep the fluid warm to ensure that the sperms didn't perish before they could reach their intended destination. I hardly noticed the busy morning traffic on the dual carriageway. Usually, the noise of the cars and the smell of exhaust fumes really bothered me, but all I could think about was whether the little pot clasped inside my protective hand might actually contain the one sperm which might become my baby.

I paused for a moment with my hand on the door before I entered the gynaecology ward at my local hospital, where I was a Ward Sister, noticing the immediate hit of warmth and familiar medicinal smells, and the sound of the patients' call bells buzzing insistently as I walked down the short corridor to the nurses' office. I greeted the two nurses who had already arrived for the day shift.

"Is it today?" asked Theresa, one of the staff nurses, her eyes lighting up.

"Yes," I said as I patted my pocket, attempting a wobbly smile. I now had the little pot of semen tucked into the pocket of my nurse's uniform, still keeping it warm.

"How exciting!" Theresa exclaimed with a beaming smile.

"Hmmmm..." I answered, unable to agree wholeheartedly that it was exciting. I felt more embarrassed than excited that my infertility problems were such public knowledge amongst my work colleagues. Mr Richmond, the Gynaecology Consultant colleague who had been investigating my inability to get pregnant, entered the office in his usual energetic whirl, a huge grin on his face. I could feel my pulse thumping in my throat.

"Ready?" he asked, rubbing his hands together briskly, as though he was about to do something exciting.

"Yes..." I replied, patting my uniform pocket again. I followed Mr Richmond into the examination room and locked the door behind me.

The consultant waited outside the privacy screen as I removed my underwear and got up onto the couch. I'd made sure that I was wearing nice underwear, had shaved my legs and had freshly painted bright red toenails – ironically the things you might do in preparation for undressing in front of a lover, but for me just ways to reduce the anxiety I felt about the prospect of exposing my body to the doctor. I could hear him moving pieces of equipment around on the trolley which I had prepared for him prior to the procedure. I placed a small blanket over my legs, took a couple of deep breaths, and told Mr Richmond that I was ready.

I covered my face with my hands rather than watch my familiar colleague in between my legs whilst he injected the semen sample directly into my uterus. The sudden sharp and gripping pain which started low in my pelvis soon removed my focus away from feeling embarrassed. I closed my eyes and held my breath as I waited for the pain to subside. It felt like the worst period cramps I had ever experienced.

"Okay, Sister – I'll see you on the ward round!" said Mr Richmond, pulling the dignity blanket back down to cover my lower body, while grinning. I knew him well enough to know that he was trying to put me at ease with his humorous tone of voice, and I also knew that he was probably using humour to cope with his own element of embarrassment.

I was still in pain and wanted to remain lying on the couch, but I knew that Mr Richmond would already be waiting in the office for me to accompany him on the ward round, so I quickly got dressed and started to clear away the examination trolley. As I started doing this, I noticed a strange feeling of being almost disconnected from myself, as though I was outside my body and watching myself. I was simply performing a familiar nursing task, one which I did on a daily basis at work, clearing away equipment after a doctor had performed a vaginal procedure, but the equipment had been used in my own body. I was both the patient and the nurse simultaneously. The boundaries between the personal and the professional felt very blurred.

I returned to the office and collected the patients' medical records trolley, letting out a slow breath when I saw that none of the nurses were there. I felt relieved that I didn't have to speak to them. I accompanied Mr Richmond as he did his ward round.

"Good morning, Mrs Townsend! How are you doing?" Mr Richmond asked the first patient on the round. "Sister – can I have her notes, please?"

I would normally have had her notes already in my hand, trying to be super-efficient and helpful, but I was struggling to maintain a professional demeanour, distracted by waves of vice-like pain spreading through my pelvis. I could feel that the blood had drained from my face, as though I was about to faint.

"Sorry," I muttered, quickly finding the patient's notes and handing them over.

I inhaled deeply a couple of times and tried to ignore the pain, pasting a smile on my pale face for the patient's benefit. Somehow, I managed to get through the ward round, and reassured myself that all the pain and embarrassment would be worth it if I actually became pregnant.

2

It's a Family Affair

(Sly and The Family Stone 1971)

I had always wanted to be a mother. Or to be more precise, I think that I had simply imagined that one day I would experience the miracle of pregnancy. I don't believe that I'd thought too much about actually being a mother, other than to have a vague mental picture of myself holding a new-born baby, like some kind of beatific Madonna. As a teenager, I was obsessed with learning about conception, and I would study in wonder about how a fetus develops within a woman's body. Whilst my school friends were reading magazines about pop stars and fashion, each month I would eagerly anticipate buying a magazine called 'Parents', and I would devour information about pregnancy, childbirth and babies. I laugh at myself as I think about this now, and I think that it's no wonder I often felt that I didn't quite fit in at school. My peers probably thought I was a bit of a weirdo! When I was fourteen years old, I began to beg my mother to have another baby. I know that it would probably be more usual for a teenager to be horrified at the prospect of their parents having another baby, not least of all due to the cringingly awful embarrassment at the idea of their parents actually having sex. My mother declined to grant my wishes.

Despite my yearnings to become pregnant sometime in the future, I was always very conscientious about contraception. The first time I had sex at the age of sixteen, with my steady boyfriend, David, was a thrilling and loving experience, although we realised straight afterwards that the condom had split, probably due to our ineptitude at using it, so we spent a couple of days in a state of high anxiety, eventually much relieved on the day my period started. On that day, I attended a local family planning clinic and I started taking the contraceptive pill. And from that day until eight years later I never missed a single pill. My student nursing days were wonderful fun-filled times – we partied most nights, and much consumption of alcohol was involved, but no matter how intoxicated I might have been on occasion, I would always check my pill pack the next morning and find that I had actually remembered to take it.

I started training as a nurse in 1979. Although my parents, Maeve and Tom, and my sister Sinead, lived very near to the hospital, I decided to move into the nurses' home, as I wanted to live independently. My younger brother had already left home. I hardly saw my parents, or my sister, for the first couple of years. It was only in hindsight that I realised that this was actually a little strange, and was perhaps indicative of the lack of real closeness between us as a family. We didn't argue, but I never felt the need to see my family, and presumably they didn't feel the need to see me either. This did not seem strange to me at the time, the feeling of disconnection between us seemed normal. I have subsequently gained a deep understanding and genuine compassion for both my mother and my father. I can comprehend how their childhood experiences would have shaped them and impacted on their ability to parent, just as my own experience has impacted on my ability to mother my own children. When I talk about how I have been shaped by my experiences as a child, I do so truly without apportioning blame. My parents were good people who got many things right too, doing the best that they were capable of with the emotional resources they had. I believe that they gave me much to be grateful for.

I was thrilled to have been accepted onto the nurse training course, but the route towards achieving this had not been straightforward. My earliest thoughts about becoming a nurse were not in any way altruistic. They were born through a sense of curiosity. When I was ten years old, one of my friends had his appendix removed, and as my parents were friends of his parents, we went to visit him in the hospital. I can still remember the smell of the hospital – a strange mixture of boiled cabbage and cleaning fluid. It seemed to me to be a place of many mysteries where all manner of interesting things might take place. Sometimes, even now, if I am walking through the older parts of the same hospital, I catch a tiny waft of that same smell and it can immediately take my mind back to those feelings of excitement and intrigue.

There was a male patient in the next bed to my friend, whose leg was suspended in the air with a metal rod through his shin. I know now that this was skeletal traction, but at the time I was utterly fascinated and had to concentrate very hard to avoid staring at his leg, for fear of being rude. I was desperate to be able to go over and take a very close look at this interesting metal rod that pierced his skin. After my little friend had his stitches taken out, he gave them to me as a gift in a small matchbox. I would look at these stitches frequently – in awe that they had actually been in his skin. I know, again I probably seem a little odd, but I believe that this episode triggered in me the first stirrings of a desire to be involved in learning more about the human body and working in a hospital.

At the time I started my training, the required level of qualification for entrance to the training course was five O-levels. Unfortunately, for various reasons, I hadn't achieved these qualifications. I left school with just one 'O' level in English and one 'O' level equivalent in French. Although in my earlier years at school I had performed well and was bright, I didn't engage well at secondary school. I was in a mixed ability class, and as I recall, it seemed that most of the teachers' time was spent trying to discipline and control a group of rowdy boys. I remember once seeing a boy throw a chair at a teacher. I never felt calm or safe at school, and I switched off. I was often bullied by some of the boys because I was so tall and skinny. I was the last girl in my class to need to wear a bra, and some of the boys would drag me into the store cupboard, pretending that they were going to cop a feel of my breasts, but then they would laugh at me as they threw me out, saying I was a waste of time because I was too flat-chested. On one occasion though, two of the less popular boys, who had been quietly witnessing the bullying, turned up at my house with a David Essex album for me, saying that they had saved up their pocket money to buy it for me because they could see that I was sad and they wanted to cheer me up. I will never forget their kindness, and often think of how such a seemingly small kind gesture can have such a hugely beneficial impact on a person – and be remembered for a lifetime.

I realise in retrospect that a contributing factor towards my disengagement was in all likelihood connected to the fact that I was in a state of deep psychological distress at that time. For two years from the age of eleven, along with one of my friends, I was being sexually abused by a neighbour, a man who was the father of one of my childhood friends. I used to lie in bed crying at night, not knowing how to extricate myself from the situation I was in, but too terrified to tell anyone for fear of the consequences. One night, when my mother was at work, my father heard me crying, and asked me what was wrong. I could no longer contain the terrible secret, so I told him what had been happening.

The neighbour had initially started giving my friend and me small amounts of money for sweets. We were used to going into his house as his son was the same age as us, and the boy's mother would sometimes invite us into their home and give us biscuits or fruit squash. My friend and I thought that it was great fun having money to buy our sweets, but we must have known that it was wrong as we used to pretend to our parents that my friend's aunt had given us the money.

The neighbour gradually progressed to showing my friend and me pornographic magazines and then forcing us to masturbate him to ejaculation. I couldn't bear to actually touch his penis with my bare hands, so I used to keep a pair of mittens on when I masturbated him – red nylon mittens with a white fur trim. I threw those filthy mittens in a river after the abuse was over. The abuser used to kiss my friend and me and ask to look at our genitals. Even now the memory of his horrible slimy mouth and disgusting foul-smelling breath makes me shudder. It was at the point where the abuser asked if he could touch my vulva with his penis that I began to get really scared and I would cry at night.

My father's response when I told him was simply to tell me not to go into the neighbour's house again. My father did tell my friend's parents about the abuse, and I was terrified that I would get her into trouble by sharing our secret, but her parents also took no action other than telling her not to go into the neighbour's house again. I spent many years after that feeling ashamed of myself, and fearing that I would be punished in some way – I was left with the belief that the abuser must have known that I was a bad person, otherwise he wouldn't have chosen me. It is a common response for an abused child to develop the false belief that they are somehow responsible for the abuse, to be left carrying a burden of misplaced shame. I used to look fearfully in the local newspaper each week to see if there was anything in there about what had happened, and if ever I saw a police car, I used to automatically turn my head away as though I was guilty of some wrongdoing. Even now as an adult, there is always a split-second pause when I see a police car and I tell myself that I don't have to look away as I haven't done anything wrong. It didn't occur to me when I was a teenager that it was strange that my parents hadn't notified the police about the abuse, or that I had never even had one single conversation about it with my mother.

The first flicker of insight about the significance and impact of the abuse occurred many years later whilst I was training to be a counsellor. I had been counselling a man who had been in prison for sexually abusing his fourteen your old step-daughter. I was discussing this client with my counselling supervisor and he commented on how emotionally cut-off I seemed to be about the fact that the client was a paedophile. My supervisor explored this further with me and I disclosed to him my own experience of being sexually abused. As I told him the story, I remember saying that maybe my own experience wasn't that bad – that at least my abuser hadn't raped me. I was minimising it in an attempt to manage my feelings about what had happened. The supervisor then asked me to picture any young female child that I might know, who was currently around the same age as I had been at the time of the abuse, and then to imagine her in the same scenario with my abuser as I had been. I immediately imagined the daughter of one of my neighbours, who was eleven years old – just a little girl – being made to do what I'd been made to do. The sudden horror of that appalling image shocked me, and for the first time I began to acknowledge the reality of what had happened to me.

When I looked at this experience from the perspective of an adult, and as a mother, I began to understand just how disconnected from each other my parents and I must have been. I imagined how I would have reacted with absolutely pure and wild rage if anyone had ever abused one of my own children. When, as an adult, I asked my father why he or my mother had never informed the police, his reply was to tell me that they hadn't wanted to upset the neighbour's family. I can understand rationally that at the time when this all happened, the early seventies, people were not as well informed about the existence and impact of sexual abuse. People generally didn't speak as openly about their problems as we might do now – they kept themselves to themselves – but the clear message to me would have been that it was important never to cause upset to others, regardless of how upset I might be. My parents tended not to enquire about how I was getting on at school and were not interested in checking that I had completed my homework. So, my gradual slide into underachievement went unnoticed.

I applied for a place at sixth form college after I had failed most of my exams, thinking that perhaps I could make up for it there. However, within my first week at college I met David, a good-looking boy who had a motorbike. We started a relationship, and quite often we would pretend to our parents that we were going to college, but would actually ride off somewhere for the day, perhaps to the coast, having a wonderful time but not doing any work towards our studies. In one of my college reports, the tutor wrote that he couldn't comment about me because he had never even met me! David's and my behaviour resulted in both of us not doing well in exams at the end of the year. I left college not knowing what to do with myself, and my boyfriend had to repeat his college year.

David and I were together for three years, and are still in touch even now. We have very fond memories of those times and share much laughter about it. Neither of us has any regrets about the fun that we had, and we both eventually managed to do well in our careers, regardless of our youthful diversions.

After leaving college, I decided to take any job I could find so that I could pay for driving lessons. I assumed that my vague aspirations of becoming a nurse were no longer valid. I found a job in a factory which made stereo speakers. Although the work was simple, I remember that job as one of the best I ever experienced, as we were a close-knit team of workers and we had great fun laughing together on the production line, dancing around to pop music from the radio. After a year in this job, I found out by chance that it was possible to enter nurse training by undertaking an entrance exam if you didn't have the required five O-levels. The entrance exam was similar to an IQ test, and as there wasn't actually anything wrong with my IQ, and it was just my attitude which had been the problem thus far, I managed to pass this test easily, and was offered a training place. Once I became a student nurse, I thrived within the learning environment of the school of nursing, and I was well able to cope with the academic elements of the training course.

Not long after I started nurse training, my relationship with David ended, and I threw myself with great enthusiasm into life as a student nurse. At one of our wild parties in the nurses' home, I met Rob. I had noticed him previously at the hospital social club and thought he was very handsome, with his dark brown hair and honey coloured skin. He asked me to dance, and as he was six feet two inches tall, I felt for the first time in my life, a lack of embarrassment about my own height. I am five feet eleven inches tall, and had always felt awkward about being such a tall woman, thinking of myself as something like a giraffe if ever I was on a dance floor surrounded by people of normal height, but dancing with Rob I almost felt petite in his arms, and I absolutely loved this.

3

Too Busy Thinking About My Baby
(Marvin Gaye 1969)

Rob and I quickly settled into a relationship. We existed as a couple within a large group of friends with whom we socialised frequently. We never did spend a lot of time on our own. As time passed, it seemed to be a foregone conclusion that we would get married, although when I look back now, I can see how even in those early days of our relationship I was to some degree unsettled. I was lively and flirtatious, always sparking and connecting with people, all part of my gregarious nature. A friend of ours once told me that Rob was like a big strong house and that I was like a naughty little girl who lived inside the house, often running up the garden path to explore the world outside, but always returning to the safety of the house. I liked being this way, and if ever I berated myself with shame about my flirtatious nature, I used to reassure myself that at least I wasn't boring.

Rob and I married in 1982. I was twenty-two years old

– far too young to even know who I was, what I wanted, or what I needed in a relationship, but it's easy to see that now in hindsight. I remember that, before the wedding, I had been experiencing fleeting moments of ambivalence about committing to marriage, which manifested as a complete lack of interest or excitement about planning our wedding or choosing my dress, but I never allowed myself to dwell on these hesitations, let alone consider taking another path. I knew that Rob was a good person and I still felt affection for him. I assumed that the cooling of passion after the early days of excitedly falling in love was normal and to be expected. If ever I did allow uncomfortable thoughts to rise to the top of my conscious mind, and momentarily consider the idea of calling off or postponing the wedding, those thoughts appeared and disappeared like snowflakes landing on the palm of a warm hand. I would immediately stop that train of thought in its tracks, as the idea of hurting Rob, or letting down family and friends, was completely unthinkable to me.

The early days of our marriage were happy enough, focussing on creating our home and building our careers, and having a great social life with our many friends. Rob was working as a mental health nurse and I had started training as a midwife after qualifying as a nurse. I had an ambition to become a Sister on the gynaecology ward, as I had absolutely loved my student placement there, but a midwifery qualification was, at that time, required for the post.

I didn't particularly enjoy being a student midwife, but I was completely enthralled by being able to witness up close the miracle of pregnancy and childbirth. It was normal practice then for the midwife to take the new-born baby into a separate room soon after delivery, to examine for abnormalities and to wash the baby. These were such precious moments for me, marvelling at the sheer perfection of each baby, lost in wonder that nature creates such a flawless miracle.

Rob and I had been married for about two years when we decided to start trying to conceive a pregnancy. Suddenly, our sex life, which had gradually become far less frequent and quite mundane, became infused with an intoxicating feeling of intense excitement and expectation. Having spent many years being so conscientious about contraception, I imagined that it would mean just a few days of not taking my contraceptive pill before I would conceive. At this time, I was working in a neonatal unit and I absolutely loved being around so many tiny babies whilst I nurtured happy dreams of having my own.

The months passed and my period continued to arrive without fail every month. I knew that it could be normal for it to take up to a year or even eighteen months for a fertile couple to conceive, but after a few months without success, I began to worry that perhaps there might be a problem with one or both of us.

After a year of trying unsuccessfully, I decided to ask

one of my medical colleagues for advice. By this time, I had left my job in the neonatal unit and taken a post as a Ward Sister on the gynaecology ward, where Mr Richmond was a Consultant Gynaecologist with whom I worked closely. He offered to examine me and to arrange a pelvic scan and some blood tests, plus a semen analysis test for Rob, the results of which were all normal. After a few more months of my failing to conceive, Mr Richmond saw Rob and me together as patients in his gynaecology clinic to begin fertility investigations.

I started taking my temperature each morning and plotting the results on a chart so that I might be able to pinpoint the time of ovulation. The curves on the graph seemed to indicate that ovulation was taking place each month. We started trying to ensure that we had sex on the days just before and just after ovulation. Already, that initial excitement and hopeful sense of expectation was waning, and sex began to feel more like a chore to be endured or tolerated in the hope of conceiving, something to be timetabled in, regardless of whether we felt any sexual desire or not.

I then underwent a laparoscopy operation, which involved having a telescopic instrument inserted into my abdomen via a surgical incision, under an anaesthetic, to check my pelvic organs. During the laparoscopy some dye was injected into my uterus to find out whether or not the surgeon could see it flowing out through the ends of the fallopian tubes. I also had a hystero-salpingogram, which is a painful procedure to again check the patency of the fallopian tubes, where radio-opaque dye is inserted into the uterus and then an x-ray is taken to see whether the dye travels through the tubes into the pelvic cavity. There appeared to be no abnormalities, and both fallopian tubes were open. Mr Richmond suggested that I should take a post-coital test to see if I might have anti-sperm antibodies which could reduce my chance of becoming pregnant. This is where it all started to become rather embarrassing for me, as I had to plan an agreed date to have sex at a particular time with Rob, and then allow Mr Richmond to examine me vaginally within an hour. It felt very intrusive, but it would become even more so.

The post-coital test showed that there might be anti-sperm antibodies present, as the sample taken from around my cervix showed reduced motility (movement) of the sperms. It seemed that my body was rejecting the sperms and actually rendering them useless, even before they could enter my uterus. Mr Richmond suggested that he could try to artificially inseminate me with Rob's sperm in an attempt to bypass the anti-sperm antibodies at the cervix.

Mr Richmond's attempts to help me to become pregnant failed. I had artificial insemination five times. After the first attempt, Rob and I spent two weeks allowing ourselves to feel a little excited – willing my period not to start. But as time went on, and every month my period arrived right on cue, any belief that I'd had that the treatment would work was diminishing.

I felt very exposed, embarrassed and humiliated to be undergoing such intimate and personal treatment at my place of work. My nursing colleagues on the ward were kind and sympathetic to me, but I could sense that they were also starting to become a little embarrassed and uncomfortable around me, especially when I had still not conceived after several months of artificial insemination treatment and when conversation turned to discussions about other women who were pregnant.

One day, as I walked into the ward office, I saw my colleagues hurriedly break away from a huddle in which they had been cooing over a baby scan photo with one of the nurses who was in early pregnancy. It was as though they were not allowed to express their happiness in front of me, and their instinctive attempts to protect me were actually well founded, as I had reached a stage where I didn't really want to hear about anyone else's pregnancy because it made me feel sick with envy.

I was aware of a growing sense of loss, in that I seemed now to be unable to bear being around pregnant women or new mothers. Me, who had always been so delighted by anything connected with babies. Over time, I gradually began to isolate myself from friends and family, particularly those who were pregnant or had children. I used to make excuses to avoid important family gatherings such as weddings – sometimes even missing funerals for close family members. I regret this now, because those family events cannot be re-lived, but I really didn't know how to be around people any longer. In retrospect I can see that this is when the first seeds of depression began to take root within me.

I don't recall in detail the conversations between Rob and me about our inability to conceive naturally. I was aware that Rob was excited about the prospect of being a father and he was disappointed each time fertility treatment didn't work. I know that it was embarrassing for him to have to produce semen samples prior to each test or treatment, and he too felt the loss of privacy in our sexual relationship. I can imagine that I may not have shared many of my very negative feelings and frustrations about infertility, particularly my growing envy of and resentment towards pregnant women or mothers, because I would have felt ashamed of myself to admit to this to anyone, even my husband. In retrospect I can certainly see that our fertility problems probably marked the beginning of the wedge that grew between us.

4

Hang On In There Baby

(Johnny Bristol 1974)

My work as a nurse on a gynaecology ward became increasingly uncomfortable, since I often had to care for women who were having pregnancy related problems, including those who were having a pregnancy terminated. Although I loved my work as a gynaecology nurse, the issue of abortion was one about which I had some very ambivalent feelings. I had been brought up as a Catholic and had been taught to believe in the sanctity of life, and I did feel an innate awareness that life is profoundly precious, but as a modern woman living in sexually liberated times, I also agreed with the concept of a woman having the agency to make her own life choices. I had no qualms about sex before marriage, or having children outside marriage, and I believed that many of the teachings of the Catholic Church were archaic and even harmful. I told myself that I shouldn't hypocritically pick and choose which elements of the church ideology I accepted.

After all, I had stopped going to mass when I was fourteen years old and I no longer felt connected to the church.

So, I chose to manage my inconsistent conscientious discomfort mostly by refusing to allow myself to dwell on it, and by telling myself that, as long as I wasn't actually performing the terminations of pregnancy myself, it was perfectly acceptable for me to help the women before and after the actual procedure. Sometimes, I struggled internally with underlying surges of resentment towards those patients who were either having repeated terminations or who acknowledged that they had taken no steps to avoid a pregnancy. Life seemed so unfair to me, that some women could become pregnant so easily when they didn't want to have a baby, yet I was desperate to conceive and, so far, had not been able to.

Eventually, Mr Richmond agreed to refer me to a specialist infertility clinic in London for further investigations and treatment. By this time, I was really struggling at work. I was constantly weighed down in a depressive fog and I couldn't remember ever having been a bright and happy sociable person. I was unable to fake cheerfulness and I thought that my colleagues must be getting frustrated by my low moods. I no longer thought of myself as a likeable person, so why should other people like me? I was sleeping badly, having a lot of bad dreams, and just wanted to run away and hide from everyone.

In 1985 I decided to leave my job and look for another post in a place where I would not know anybody, a place where I could be anonymous. It seems rather odd to think about it now, but I applied and was successfully appointed to be a senior nurse in an infertility clinic in a London hospital. I had been honest and open with the interviewers about my own infertility experience, and had told them that I was on a waiting list for my first appointment at the Hammersmith Hospital. The interviewers seemed to think that my own experience would be of benefit in helping other people with infertility, because I would have a deeper insight into how the patients might feel. In some ways perhaps they were right, but I stayed in that job for only six months as everything felt too close for comfort. I did, however, meet many women who had successful in-vitro-fertilisation (IVF) treatment in our clinic, so I came away at least with a belief that IVF treatment can work, and that there was still some hope for me, if I was ever to end up having IVF myself.

Shortly after I started working in London, I'd had my first appointment with Professor Robert Winston at the Hammersmith Hospital, who had looked me directly in the eyes and reassured me very confidently that he was sure he would be able to help me to get pregnant. This positive statement from an internationally renowned fertility expert gave me a real boost of hope. I had to undergo the full range of investigations again, including another laparoscopy, another hystero-salpingogram, several scans, and a repeat of the post coital test, the results of which were all normal. Professor Winston suggested that we could try intra-uterine insemination (IUI) again, and if that wasn't successful, I would become a candidate for IVF for unexplained infertility. He put me on the NHS waiting list for IVF anyway, just in case.

During the next few months, I underwent four cycles of IUI at the Hammersmith. This time, the semen samples were treated with a process called sperm washing to remove the seminal fluid, and the insemination procedure proved to be much less painful than my previous experiences on the gynaecology ward, although it was still uncomfortable having instruments inserted into my vagina and tubes inserted through my cervix. Untreated seminal fluid contains a substance called prostaglandin, which stimulates the uterus to contract, causing period-like pains. In fact, one of the methods of inducing labour contractions is to insert a pessary that contains prostaglandin into the vagina – and there is an old-wives tale which purports that having unprotected sexual intercourse will do the same thing.

When I left my job at the fertility clinic, I decided to work as an agency nurse, because this would allow me the flexibility to take time off for fertility treatments. This proved to be a wise decision. I found myself having to travel up and down to the Hammersmith Hospital, a ninety-minute journey each way, several times each month. I became an expert at filling my bladder, and being able to maintain an uncomfortably full bladder for long periods of time, prior to each scan. For every cycle in which I was having IUI, I needed to have five or six scans in order to track the development of an egg-containing follicle on my ovary, and to pinpoint exactly when to have the IUI. Working as an agency nurse, I appreciated the relative anonymity of not knowing my work colleagues, because I could maintain a degree of privacy about my infertility treatments.

Despite all of our efforts, I didn't manage to conceive after four cycles of IUI. I was so tired and I was becoming increasingly depressed, but not yet ready to give up on my mission to become a mother. The fertility clinic doctors suggested that I should stop the IUI treatments and await IVF. The waiting list was approximately one year on the NHS, but time was on my side as I was only 28 years old. I carried on working as an agency nurse, maintained a distance from my friends and family, and kept my head down whilst I waited.

5

I Say a Little Prayer

(Aretha Franklin 1968)

Eventually, in January 1989, five years after my infertility investigations and treatment had begun, I started IVF treatment. This involved several weeks of injecting myself with hormone blocking drugs to stop my natural menstrual cycle, effectively putting me into a sudden artificial menopause, then injecting a different drug to stimulate my ovaries to produce an excess of egg-containing follicles, and repeatedly travelling up and down to the Hammersmith hospital in London for ultrasound scans. The regime of hormones played havoc with my mood, and my abdomen was distended and uncomfortable due to the hyper-stimulation of my ovaries, but I coped well with this in the excitement of finally having treatment which might give me a good chance of becoming pregnant. I responded well to the hormone injections and an ultrasound scan showed that my ovaries had developed an abundance of follicles. Sixteen eggs were collected during an uncomfortable procedure in which a long needle was inserted into the top of my vagina to withdraw the eggs under ultrasound guidance. Of the sixteen eggs, six had fertilised and produced healthy looking embryos when they were added to Rob's sperm.

On the planned day for embryo transfer, Rob and I sat in the fertility clinic waiting room. After discussion with the doctor, we had agreed to have three embryos implanted, although we were advised that this could result in a multiple pregnancy which might carry additional risks, such as premature birth. At the time I would have foolishly consented if it had been suggested that all six embryos were transferred – I was so desperate to maximise my chances of becoming pregnant. Rob and I were asked if we would consent to the remaining three embryos being used for research at the hospital. We felt rather sad about this, but as we didn't have the option of freezing the embryos at that time, and because we knew that our IVF treatment had only been possible as a result of all the infertility research that had gone before, we felt that we had a moral duty to consent.

"Do you think this is it?" asked Rob, taking my hand in his and looking at me with hope in his eyes.

"I think so," I said. "The rate of success of IVF is around 25% for a woman of my age. There are three other women in this waiting room – and I am going to be the one in four who gets pregnant!"

As we were giggling at my statement of intent, the doctor called us in to the treatment room. Once more I took up my, by now very familiar, position of lying on a gynaecology couch with my legs wide apart in stirrups. I remember that the room was quite dark and there was gentle music playing. The doctor and his assistant nurse spoke softly, and I smiled to myself as I thought about how one might dim the lights and play soft music as a romantic prelude to making love. This medical procedure was as far removed from a romantic conception as it was possible to be, but I suppose the low lighting and quiet atmosphere did help me to relax a little.

Rob sat at the head end of the table and held my hand. Appreciative that he was allowed to be with me during the procedure, I allowed myself to fantasise about a future day when Rob would be sitting at the head of a different bed, holding my hand and supporting me as I gave birth to our baby.

As the doctor gently inserted the three fertilised embryos into my womb, I focussed clearly on visualising these little embryos settling in and finding a nice warm place to implant, almost as though they might be breathing a sigh of relief on returning to my body after spending their first days of existence in a London hospital laboratory.

Rob and I held hands as we walked out of the clinic with a new spring in our step. We were excited, but also nervous about holding out too much hope. It was difficult to know how to feel. If we were too excited, then the disappointment of our failure to conceive might be even harder to cope with, but I had a strong sense that I needed to maintain a positive and welcoming energy in my body, as though by imagining myself pregnant I could manifest it.

"What if it doesn't work?" Rob said.

"Don't forget – one in four!! And I am the one in four!" I reminded Rob as we drove back home, preparing ourselves mentally for a two-week wait to find out whether or not I was pregnant.

During the fortnight after embryo transfer, I compulsively analysed all my bodily sensations from morning until night. Was that a twinge of nausea I just felt? Was the discomfort in my breasts any different from the usual pre-menstrual aching? I didn't initially feel any different from usual, but as I neared the end of the two weeks, I realised that I wasn't experiencing the low ache in my pelvis which typically tended to herald the onset of a period. I wasn't sure whether this was a good or a bad sign, but I was optimistic, being aware from my previous experience of working in a fertility clinic, that very often when treatment had been unsuccessful, the women would start to menstruate a few days before the end of the two weeks. Could the fact that I wasn't bleeding possibly mean that I was in fact pregnant? I hardly dared to allow myself to feel excited.

On day fourteen after the embryo transfer, I was awake at

sunrise and spent a couple of hours pacing around the house, waiting for the time when I knew that the fertility clinic would be open so that I could phone them for the results of a blood test I'd had taken the previous day to determine whether or not I was pregnant. Unfortunately, Rob was working away from home and he had been unable to take the day off work at short notice.

At exactly nine am, I sat on the edge of the bed, my hands shaking as I dialled the number of the clinic.

"Hello...is that the fertility clinic?" I asked, my voice thin with anxiety. "I'm phoning for my blood test results from yesterday."

"Ok. What's your name and date of birth?" a woman replied in a matter-of-fact tone of voice which didn't quite seem to match the magnitude of my enquiry.

I gave the requested details and the woman asked me to hold the line for a moment.

I held my breath and sat in suspended animation, as still as a stone, whilst I waited for her to come back onto the line.

"Good news!" the woman said. "You're pregnant!"

I didn't really hear anything much of what she said after that. I felt as though my body was being washed away by an amazing flood of relief as I flopped down onto the bed. My heart was bursting with sheer joy. I wanted to shout and scream, to tell everybody my news, but first I phoned Rob at work and told him. I felt very sad then that he had not been able to be with me at such a precious moment, but it was still so lovely to hear his delighted expressions of absolute joy and relief mirroring my own. On reflection, I also think now it's rather sad that if I'd received bad news that day and had been told that I wasn't pregnant, then I would have been alone and unsupported in that moment. However, I had always been used to being resolutely self-sufficient, so it hadn't occurred to me to push for Rob to miss work on that day.

Then, I did something which seems quite odd in retrospect. Without even thinking about it, and before I told anyone else the good news, I went straight to the Catholic church that I had attended as a child and I offered prayers of gratitude for the miracle of my pregnancy. I can remember a distinct feeling of being somehow forgiven, and that maybe, by allowing me to become pregnant, God had absolved me of any misdoings in my life. It fascinates me now to think that I must have been unconsciously carrying a heavy weight of guilt and perhaps an innate sense that I was, in some way, a bad person. Had I somehow subconsciously thought that my years of infertility were a punishment?

Two weeks after the pregnancy test, Rob and I attended the fertility clinic for a scan. I had been going to the toilet frequently and checking for any sign of vaginal bleeding which might have heralded the start of an early miscarriage, but so far there had not been even a tiny speck of blood.

"What if there are three of them in there?" asked Rob as

we waited to be called in.

"That would be fantastic!!" I replied. "The more the merrier!" I naively quipped.

Once again, I found myself laying on my back on a gynaecology couch with my legs open whilst the doctor inserted the trans-vaginal scan probe into my vagina. By now, I'd had so many intimate examinations and procedures that I no longer registered any embarrassment. Besides, I was far too excited at that moment to worry about that.

For what seemed like an age, the doctor manoeuvred the probe around, looking at the scanner screen, whilst we were waiting for him to speak. Rob was holding my hand, stroking my sweaty palm as we shared anxious glances – absolutely dreading that the doctor might tell us that the pregnancy wasn't viable.

Eventually, he turned the screen around towards us and said, "Look – what can you see there?"

As a gynaecology nurse, I was familiar with what a scan image of early pregnancy looks like, and I could see two distinct dark circular areas amidst the white shadow image of my uterus.

"Er…are there…two?" I tentatively asked.

"Yes – you are having twins!! The doctor replied." And everything looks absolutely fine…look…you can see their hearts beating!" the doctor said as he pointed to the screen.

Rob and I were absolutely thrilled at this news –

incredulous at our good fortune and high with the relief of knowing that, after all that we had been through in trying to achieve a pregnancy, we really were at last going to be parents. We kept looking at each other and laughing with utter joy. The two of us practically skipped out of the clinic, holding hands and with beaming smiles, clutching some photographs which the doctor had given to us of the scan images of the twins, plus a couple of pictures of the three embryos taken at the stage of just two cell divisions, just after fertilisation had occurred. If ever my house was on fire, those photos would be the first things I would run to save.

6

Best Thing That Ever Happened to Me

(Gladys Knight And The Pips 1973)

I absolutely loved being pregnant. It was every bit as wonderful as I had imagined it would be. I felt well the entire time, full of energy, and if ever I did notice a tiny bit of morning sickness, I revelled in it, as I took it as a sign that I had plenty of pregnancy hormones circulating in my body. Rob and I had started telling all our family and friends immediately after I'd had the positive test. Some people believe that it is unwise to tell people too early in case the pregnancy miscarries, but I was so delighted with myself that I just had to share the news. I figured that even if things did go wrong, at least Rob and I would have had this little bit of time when we could celebrate joyously. It was a wonderful thing to see the reactions of joy and relief on the faces of all the people in our lives who had been witness to our struggle with infertility – I had imagined these happy scenes as a fantasy for so long. As the pregnancy progressed, I felt a thrill with every little flutter and kick as the twins moved around inside my womb. I used to feel them reacting to each other – one would kick out and then the other would retaliate with a push. I pictured them vying for space within me and it made Rob and me laugh – as though our children were squabbling before they had even been born! I told everyone I met that I was expecting twins, and had no qualms about encouraging anyone and everyone to place a hand on my magnificent bump. I grew huge as the twins were growing healthily, but I was easily able to carry the weight and the size of them as I am so tall.

Once I'd had my first scan, I felt relaxed and confident about the pregnancy, but there was one small shadow which lurked at the edge of my awareness. From time to time, I would allow my thoughts to drift back to the experience of IVF. I didn't want to dwell on this – I just wanted to delight in being pregnant – to be a normal woman, able to join in with all the social events with family and friends and now able to genuinely celebrate other women's pregnancies too. However, it occurred to me one day to question how sure I could be that the babies growing inside me were actually mine and Rob's babies? After all, their conception had occurred in a laboratory – and what if the doctor had picked up the wrong petri-dish and implanted someone else's embryos in my uterus? I knew that there were protocols in place to reduce the risk of this type of disastrous error ever occurring, but I also knew that sometimes human beings can make mistakes.

I had read stories about such events occurring. I had no way of being able to definitively answer this question until after the twins were born, so I just had to hope that the babies I was carrying were mine. I managed most of the time to put these niggling worries to the back of my mind. I didn't discuss my concerns with Rob, and the bond of love for my unborn babies became stronger each day.

Rob was working away from home for most of the pregnancy, but I felt perfectly happy by myself. I found that I didn't really miss him as much as I might have expected. I was so focussed on myself, and still feeling this strange sense of relief – that I was now a good person and all was well in my world. I realise that this might all sound a bit melodramatic, but I can remember a feeling of being in some way cured of my somehow 'dangerous' sexual nature, and I mused about how I might now be more aligned with the archetype of the Madonna than the whore. I learned more about the roots to these thoughts many years later – not least that some of my innate sense of being somehow 'bad' was a legacy of the traumatic experience of being sexually abused in my early teenage years.

I worked as an agency nurse until the 24th week of my pregnancy, and I then spent a few wonderful weeks relaxing and preparing for the arrival of the twins. I revelled in being able to spend many happy hours organising the cupboards and chest of drawers in what was to become the nursery room – thrilled to be folding tiny articles of baby clothing into neat little piles and stacking up the nappies. Even now the baby-powder smell of plastic nappy-sacks takes me right back there.

In October 1989, at thirty-six weeks into the pregnancy, I started having occasional mild sensations of abdominal tightening, which I assumed were just the normal Braxton Hicks contractions. I mentioned this to Mr Richmond at my antenatal clinic appointment.

"Well, I think perhaps I should examine you then," said Mr Richmond.

He finished the vaginal examination and then stepped back from the couch with an amused look on his face as he snapped his examination gloves off.

"You're going to have these babies either tonight or tomorrow! You're three centimetres dilated!"

I was very surprised, since I hadn't really experienced any labour pains yet. Rob and I went home with a plan to return to the hospital in the morning for an epidural, if I hadn't needed to go in overnight.

The next morning, I still wasn't feeling anything other than mild irregular uterine contractions which were not at all painful. Mr Richmond examined me again and told me that my cervix was now four centimetres dilated. The anaesthetist inserted an epidural catheter into my spine, an intravenous infusion was started to stimulate contractions, and I sat on the bed happily pain free for the next three hours, high with excitement that Rob and I would soon meet our babies.

By the time my cervix reached ten centimetres dilation, the epidural had worn off and I could feel the uterine contractions urging me to push. I still didn't experience this as pain, and actually enjoyed the sensation of bearing down with each wave of pressure. I had been pushing hard for about an hour when the midwife asked to examine me internally.

"Twin one doesn't seem to be moving at all – despite all of your hard work," said the midwife. "The fetal monitor trace seems to be ok for both babies, but I think I'll ask Mr Richmond to come and assess you."

"So, what's going on here then?" asked Mr Richmond as he entered the room a few minutes later. "Let's take a look, shall we?"

He proceeded to examine me, and I expected him to tell me that all was fine.

"Twin one's decided to get his or her head stuck in a transverse position, so I'm going to need to use forceps to turn baby's head into the right position for delivery," said Mr Richmond, seemingly with confidence.

He turned to the midwife, saying, "Sister, get me Keilland's and Neville Barnes forceps, please."

My heart sank and I started to feel frightened because suddenly everything seemed to be going wrong. I knew from my midwifery experience that Kielland's rotation forceps were very rarely used any more, as caesarean section was the preferred safer option if a baby needed to be delivered quickly. The use of these long straight forceps to rotate a baby's head when stuck in a transverse position was an almost obsolete skill which most modern obstetricians no longer needed. I knew that Mr Richmond was an older and very experienced obstetrician, so I had to trust that he knew what he was doing. I regretfully imagined the first twin's head being crushed against my unyielding pelvis every time I'd pushed so hard in the preceding hour. I could hear the bleeping of the fetal heart monitors, and every time I heard a slight deceleration in the babies' heart rates, a surge of adrenaline-fuelled terror coursed through my body.

There was no time for the epidural to be topped up, so when Mr Richmond inserted the Kielland's forceps, I thought I was going to pass out with the sudden shock of intense pain. He managed to turn twin one's head using the forceps, and then had to insert another pair of curved forceps to deliver the first twin through the birth canal. To my enormous relief I heard the baby, a girl, start to cry as the midwife took her and wrapped her in a pink blanket. She placed Evie in my arms, and I remember a brief lull in my anxiety levels as I could immediately see that her face looked just like mine did in photographs of me as a baby. At that moment I knew that she was indeed my own child, but I couldn't relax and enjoy the wonder at my new little girl, as I still had another baby to be delivered.

Mr Richmond examined me again and informed Rob and me that unfortunately, twin two had decided to make the most of the extra room inside my uterus and got him- or herself into a position where their whole body was lying in a horizontal position inside my womb. It would not have been possible for the baby to be delivered vaginally in that position. I was vaguely aware by that point that the room was beginning to fill up with several more people – anaesthetists, paediatricians and more midwives on standby, should they be needed. The air was hot and moist, and sweat was dripping from my forehead due to the heat in the room and my fear. Rob tried to wipe my forehead with a cool cloth to help me, but I brushed him away in frustration.

"Sister, get theatre ready for c-section," I heard Mr Richmond instruct one of the midwives, and although his voice seemed calm, I could see a red flush creeping up his neck, exposing his own fear and signalling to me that he was now seriously nervous. That was the moment when I really began to panic and my level of anxiety ramped up to abject terror. I knew that there was a risk to the second twin at this point due to a potential lack of oxygen if the baby wasn't delivered very quickly, and I immediately catastrophised with visions of my baby ending up with cerebral palsy, or maybe not even surviving at all.

I squeezed Rob's hand and let out a guttural "Fuck!" as

another shock of pain bore through me when Mr Richmond inserted his lower arm inside my vagina, whilst at the same time he asked a midwife to apply external pressure to my abdomen. As Mr Richmond moved his arm around inside me, trying to manoeuvre the second twin into a good position for delivery, I remember thinking that it seemed like something I'd seen vets do on television with farm animals struggling in obstructed labour.

"Ok, I've got the feet," said Mr Richmond, and he proceeded to deliver the second twin, by breech, using yet another set of forceps to deliver his head.

"You have a boy!" Mr Richmond pronounced as he held Daniel up like a slick and bloodied trophy for me to see. It was a few seconds before Daniel let out a healthy wail, and when the midwife held him near me so that I could see his face, I immediately recognised, with great relief, that his tiny face looked exactly like Rob's.

That evening, up on the post-natal ward, after Rob had gone home, I was lying on the bed, hardly able to believe that I was still alive after what my body had been through. I looked at my beautiful babies sleeping peacefully in their little Perspex cots and felt connected to all women since the beginning of time that had ever given birth. I was now, at last, a mother – part of this ancestral thread of mothers, an ancient lineage, since the very beginning of human life on earth. I wondered if that might be what the phrase 'in the club' meant?

I was in hospital for a week, as it was considered that I would need some time and support after such a traumatic instrumental delivery. It wasn't an easy week. I was in a lot of pain, finding it hard to sit in a chair or on the bed, and trying very hard to establish breast-feeding Evie and Daniel. They were very hungry babies, weighing in at six pounds each, even though they were born a month early, and I spent most of my days tentatively sitting on the edge of a chair with a baby on each breast simultaneously, feeding continuously. I didn't get much privacy, as word had got round that the IVF twins had been born, so I had a constant stream of visitors, including family, friends, current and ex-colleagues, and even one of the domestic staff from the main hospital whose friend worked on the post-natal ward and had told her that she should come and see these cute twins! I just wanted to be by myself, learning to care for my new-born babies, but it didn't occur to me to say no to visits – I would have considered that to be very impolite. My ingrained need to never disappoint anyone and to be liked by everyone outweighed my need for privacy.

7

It Takes Two

(Marvin Gaye and Kim Weston 1966)

Once I was home with the twins, Rob went back to work, and the reality of motherhood began to bite. Evie and Daniel seemed to cry all the time, wanting to feed constantly. I was still trying to breast feed them, but I was beginning to think that maybe I wasn't producing enough milk. I tried to seek help and advice from my Health Visitor, but unfortunately, in taking her advice to supplement with bottle feeding, I actually reduced my own breast milk supply even further.

I remember sometimes thinking at that time that I wished I had a mother – someone who could guide me and support me through the early days of mothering. The strange thing is that I actually did have a mother, who lived very near to us, but she was drinking very heavily and descending further into alcoholism. She didn't seem to be at all interested in me or my babies. There was no real relationship between us, so to all intent and purposes I felt that I was motherless. I had no expectation that my father might be able to help me because he was too embroiled in his daily struggle to cope with my mother's alcoholism.

I stopped breast feeding when Evie and Daniel were three weeks old. I was utterly exhausted, bone weary from constant feeding day and night, and my nipples were so raw that they were bleeding. I felt certain now that I wasn't producing enough milk for them, as it seemed to me that they were crying and unsettled most of the time. I was absolutely crestfallen about making this decision, because I had desperately wanted to breast feed my babies, to do it all perfectly, to be the earth-mother I had, quite mistakenly, always imagined I would be. I remember standing in the shower on the last day that I breastfed the twins, crying as I watched milk trickling from my nipples, and thinking that it was almost as though my body was crying too. I grieved for a long time about my failure to establish breast feeding – and sometimes even now will notice a little pang of sadness when I see a baby being breast fed.

After a couple of weeks of fully bottle-feeding, I realised that there didn't seem to be much reduction in the babies' crying. It occurred to me then, that, individually, they probably weren't crying excessively compared to other babies, but as there was always one or the other of them crying, I was constantly experiencing a primal response to the sound of it. Nature has ensured that a baby's cry triggers in the mother an innate feeling of anxiety and an immediate imperative to comfort and soothe, usually by feeding. It's one of nature's ways of making sure that babies survive. The mother feels relief and contentment when her baby is settled and content, but I seemed never to be able to achieve that lovely peaceful feeling. I was permanently on high alert. Whilst I was feeding one twin, the other one would be crying. Then I would be feeding the second twin, and the one I'd just fed and put down would be crying with wind, a wet nappy, or a little vomiting. What I really needed was to have someone around to help and support me, but Rob was too busy, working overtime to pay for the additional expense of the double requirement of nappies and formula milk, and there was nobody else to ask. I did have friends, and my sister Sinead, who came to see me and the twins for short visits, but they were either working or managing whatever was going on in their own lives, so I didn't feel that I could ask them for any more support than they were able to give. At one point, I found out from the local twin club that a nearby college was looking for mothers who would allow a nursery nurse student to spend time with them and their babies as part of their learning, so I contacted the college. For a few weeks, a young woman called Hayley used to come to the house once each week for a couple of hours, and together we would just play with Evie and Dan and I would teach her how to care for a baby. Having Hayley there was helpful to me in some ways, but I always wished that I had someone to whom I was close, rather than a stranger, helping me. I wasn't allowed, and could never have relaxed enough, to leave Hayley unsupervised with the twins, so it didn't really give me a break.

When I reflect now on this part of my life, and the traumatic delivery of my babies in particular, I find it hard to understand how I had allowed my labour to be medically managed to the extent that it was. As a tall woman with a probably quite roomy pelvis, I imagine that I perhaps might have been able to deliver two six-pound babies very easily if I had allowed my labour to continue as naturally as it had begun. After all, I had got to four centimetres dilation without any discomfort at all, but I had then surrendered myself to the obstetrician's authority and obeyed him without question. I would not have dreamed of making a fuss and asserting my own authority, for fear that I might in some way be endangering my babies if I didn't follow the doctor's advice. I don't think I would have even considered back then that I could have any agency about influencing the course of my own labour. Fortunately, many things have changed in the way labour is managed since those days more than thirty years ago. It is a sad reflection that, when I was training to be a midwife, some obstetricians and midwives either explicitly or indirectly held the rather negative opinion that women who were particularly vocal about what they did and didn't want to happen during their labour were pushy and awkward trouble makers. Women are now much more readily encouraged to create a birth plan and they are supported in their personal choices regarding where and how they give birth to their babies, safety permitting.

I wonder now whether perhaps, if I had remained mobile and not allowed myself to be strapped to a bed with an epidural and an intravenous infusion, things might have been very different. I will never know, but I do still feel disappointed that my experience of such a traumatic delivery left me in a state of shock for many months, both physically and mentally, which really did impact on my ability to cope with twins as a first-time mother.

What I do know is that I don't have many memories of experiencing real joy during the first few months of Evie's and Daniel's lives. During the five years of infertility, I had built up such an idealised picture of how I would be as a mother. The reality of the sheer hard work and exhaustion of new motherhood is always something for which no woman can be fully prepared, but I was completely unable to express with any degree of honesty any of my negative thoughts, for fear that I might be considered ungrateful. After all, I had been fortunate enough to have had two beautiful and healthy twins, a boy and a girl, through my first attempt at IVF treatment – and I was grateful. I would gaze at my babies and feel my heart absolutely swelling with love for them in their innocence and perfection – but I seemed to be unable to relax or feel completely happy for more than an occasional moment. Research has shown that women who have experienced fertility treatments might paradoxically have an increased risk of post-natal depression, probably due to the repression of the normal mixed-up emotions that can arise after the hormonal storm of childbirth.

I survived those early months by taking the twins out in their pushchair for long walks each day in between feeds. They tended to sleep during these walks, and it was a relief to have some respite from the crying. To get through the days, I used to walk up to the local hospital and visit the lovely old ladies who volunteered in the little hospital shop, enjoying how they always made such a fuss cooing over my babies, showing off how cute they looked in their little matching pink and blue outfits. These small moments of positive experience helped me to remember how beautiful Evie and Daniel were, and indeed how lucky I was to be a mother. I lost a lot of my pregnancy weight as a result of all the walking – which was a bonus!

I managed to pretend to myself and others that all was well, but in reality, I was swallowing feelings of unspecific sadness, and those early tiny seeds of depression were now tendrils of despair which were growing insidiously within me. Looking back, I believe that as a new mother I became a little more consciously aware of the disconnection between myself and my own mother, although at the time I didn't fully realise this. I just had a vague underlying feeling of sadness –

and a strange longing to be mothered, or looked after, myself. I remember having to spend a day in hospital a few weeks after the twins were born. I had a procedure under general anaesthetic to re-position my coccyx (tail bone) as it had been damaged during childbirth, and I cried when the nurse brought me a sandwich and a cup of tea post operatively because she was being so kind to me. I wished that I could stay in hospital for longer so that I could be cared for instead of always being the carer.

When the twins were around six weeks old, the issue of resuming a sexual relationship with Rob began to loom. Rob expected, not unreasonably, that once I had recovered physically from the birth, we should be able to start having sex again. It's true that by then my body had just about healed, but I still had a sense of being in a state of physical and mental shock – almost as if I had actually died in childbirth and was now some kind of facsimile of my former self. I felt absolutely no sexual desire and the prospect of sex actually began to fill me with dread. However, being true to my people-pleasing nature, I felt very guilty and uncomfortable about rejecting Rob, so I said yes to sex when I didn't want to, trying to make Rob feel better. Each time, I could feel my body tensing and freezing. I wasn't engaging in making love, I was just about managing to tolerate occasional episodes of intercourse. I neither instigated nor accepted any attempts at foreplay. I started to avoid expressing any affection towards

Rob for fear that he might perceive it as a signal that sex was on the agenda. And whenever we did have sex, it would leave me feeling angry – as though I had been somehow violated, even though I was consenting to sex, and this set up a vicious cycle of self-perpetuating mutual hostility. As a mental health nurse, Rob was wise enough to know that I might be suffering from post-natal depression, and with his encouragement I did start taking antidepressants after a consultation with my GP, but I didn't feel any better. It just numbed the angry feelings a little.

I decided to go back to work part-time when Evie and Daniel were five months old, as Rob's salary didn't quite cover our living expenses now that we had to buy double of everything for our babies. I worked as a bank nurse in a local hospital, with just one evening shift or one night shift per week at times when Rob could be at home to look after the twins. I felt much ambivalence and guilt about being away from my babies, and I can remember that at first, I had a distinct sense of something missing from my body, like missing a limb, whenever I was apart from them. I did find that having to engage with patients and colleagues at work lifted my mood a little. I began to feel a bit more like my old self, enjoying being friendly and warm to people instead of emotionally shut off in my own world. I think that these few hours of time out felt like a rest for me, and to some extent re-charged my energy levels by lifting the depression slightly, allowing me to be much more emotionally present and to enjoy being a mum much more when I was with Evie and Daniel. I started to socialise with new friends, mostly other mothers of young babies, and I have many happy memories of us proudly walking around with our babies in their pushchairs and going for picnics in the parks, sharing our stories and watching delightedly as our children developed and grew. I did find though, that going to coffee mornings with the other mothers didn't quite work for me once the twins were mobile, because, whilst the other mothers would be watching their one baby and drinking their coffee, I would be like a headless chicken running around after my two babies as they crawled off in opposite directions. I found that attending the twins club was helpful, as I learned from mothers of twins slightly older than mine about various ways to adapt to caring for two babies. After I had given up breastfeeding, I'd spent the first six months of Evie and Dan's lives trying to ensure that I always held them one at a time when I was giving them a bottle. I'd been anxious to ensure that they each had that individual time being held by me with proper eye contact – so afraid that they might feel disconnected from their mother – despite the fact that it was never a relaxing experience because the other twin would be crying and needing me too. Along with most first-time mothers, I was trying to do everything perfectly and 'by the book'. One of the twin mothers suggested that I put both twins in their bouncy chairs and fed them their bottles or their weaning foods at the same time. I did resist this for a while as it seemed wrong to me, but when eventually I did give in and try it, I found it was a revelation! I could still look at them both as I fed them, their hunger was satiated simultaneously, and so we were able to spend some happy and contented time after each feed. I gradually became a slightly more relaxed mother, which I know would have been better for my babies.

I did continue to take antidepressants, but nobody knew about this other than Rob. I didn't want to tell anyone, as I felt ashamed that I should need treatment for depression when I thought I should have been happy. After all, I had achieved my dream of becoming a mother, I had two beautiful healthy babies, I had a comfortable home, and my husband wasn't cruel to me. I remained completely disinterested in sex and was aware of feeling a permanent hidden current of anger bubbling just beneath the surface, which would manifest as short sharp bursts of temper at quite inconsequential things. Rob and I functioned quite well in practical terms as parents, but I felt very disconnected from him emotionally. The more time passed, the more deeply entrenched our disconnection felt. Neither of us was comfortable with confrontation, so we didn't discuss the chasm of coldness growing between us. I didn't know whether or not Rob was happy in our marriage, but I knew that my rejection of him sexually was upsetting him. He suggested that perhaps I might have an underlying psychosexual problem which was the cause of my complete lack of physical desire. I did briefly consider whether to try to get some help for this through counselling, but by then I had such a total lack of motivation to try to fix things that I did not want to entertain the prospect of it.

8

Tell It Like It Is

(Aaron Neville 1966)

When Evie and Daniel were two years old, I did something which many troubled people do. Rather than seek psychological help for myself, I enrolled on a counselling diploma course at a local college, telling myself that I would be a great counsellor as I had good communication skills, and I had already previously completed a year's introduction to counselling course. I'd always been interested in the psychological elements of the human experience, and I had found myself increasingly drawn to anyone who was suffering emotionally, whether it might be my friends, colleagues or patients at work. I have never been one to enjoy small talk, and my usual modus operandi at any social gathering would be to gravitate towards just one person and get into deep and meaningful conversations about feelings. I suspect now that my subconscious motivation for undertaking the course was probably really to help myself. The concept of the wounded healer is well recognised – where a person gravitates towards helping others because they are so attuned to understanding difficult emotions, having experienced their own traumas, yet are, for various reasons, unable to accept support themselves. The wounded healer's compulsive helpfulness is often a projection of their own need to be supported. I believe that this is an underlying factor for many people who are attracted to careers such as nursing and medicine. I suspect that this element of my personality partly underpinned my own choice of career as a nurse, along with my curiosity.

As part of the course, we would practise counselling with our fellow students, working with real issues in our own lives. We also had to have formal counselling for ourselves to contribute towards our learning. For the first eighteen months of my course, I mainly explored my feelings of guilt and discomfort about being a working mother. I seemed to have an enormous fear of doing anything which I thought might cause my children to feel disconnected from me. Or not loved enough. No matter how I rationalised, I couldn't seem to shake this feeling. Rob didn't seem to be feeling guilty when he was at work. I remember a conversation with one of my counselling tutors, who suggested that the modern western idea of the nuclear family, with the father working full-time and the childcare being mainly the responsibility of the mother, was actually nothing but a societal and cultural construct. She explained that in many other cultures the responsibility for childcare falls upon a whole group of people, and it is considered perfectly normal for both parents to work whilst grandparents and other relatives look after their children for them. During my early years of parenting, it used to help me a little to think that the way I had to juggle various childcare solutions with so many different people whilst I was working was really just another version of 'the child being raised by a village'.

During my counselling training I also explored my anger about my mother's dependence on alcohol. It was during this time that I first began to understand how the lack of a close relationship with my mother had affected me throughout my life. I learned a little about the theories of attachment, how, ideally, a mother and baby create an amazingly close bond so that the baby forms a secure attachment to the mother. Sometimes, for various reasons, something can impact negatively on this early bonding process, resulting in an insecure attachment. I began to have a sense that my own attachment as a baby to my mother had probably been insecure, which might have influenced my behaviour, my life choices, my relationships, and the ways in which I perceived the world around me. Through counselling, I was starting to see how my mother might have been unable to form an attachment with me as a result of her own experiences.

I was born in 1960, not very long after my mother had been forced to give up her first baby, a boy, for adoption, having become pregnant outside wedlock in Ireland in the 1950s. In Ireland at that time, predominantly a Catholic country, a young woman in my mother's situation would have been treated with appalling contempt and made to feel intense shame. My mother would have had no choice other than give up her child for adoption. I do not know much about the baby's father or my mother's relationship with him, or the way that my mother was rejected by and let down by him. I didn't think to ask her when she was alive – and now it's too late. She was sent away to live with one of her sisters in a quiet village in Ireland when she was just eight weeks pregnant – hidden away for the duration of the pregnancy. When her son was born, she remained in the hospital for two weeks after the birth. She had to breast feed him for those two weeks, before she was made to hand him over to a nun from a convent in Dublin, who would arrange for him to be adopted. She placed a small St Christopher medal on his vest before he was taken from her – a token to keep him safe on his journey through life. Not long after this terrible experience, my mother met my father. They came to England to start a new life, married in 1959, and I was born almost a year later.

As I explored my relationship with my mother during counselling, I sensed that, when I was born, she would have safely provided the physical care I needed as a tiny baby, but she was probably unable to form a close bond with me. As a mother myself, I could intuitively imagine that she would have been left with an intense weight of guilt about parting with her first-born child, and that if she had bonded with me that might have magnified her guilt about giving up her son. This is conjecture and supposition on my part – I will never know for sure – but it perhaps goes some way towards explaining our lack of closeness.

I first learned about the existence of my half-brother when I was twenty-eight years old. He had decided to search for his birth mother, and had made contact with the convent that had arranged his adoption. The convent contacted my mother's sister – she was still living in the same house – and the nun asked my aunt to let my mother know that her son wished to meet her. My mother gave me this mind-blowing piece of information one day when I called to my parents' house and found her alone at home in a very distressed state. Strangely, in a way, I was not entirely shocked. I had for a long time sensed that she was troubled about something – she used to get very tearful listening to maudlin old Irish songs about 'gentle mothers' and 'nobody's child' – and say to us all that "one day I'll write a book and then you'll all understand." My mother told me that she wanted to meet her son, but that my father knew nothing about his existence. I agreed to help to arrange a meeting, but I said that I didn't want to do it behind my father's back. Interestingly, when she told my father, he admitted that he had always known about it – rumours would have spread when a young Irish girl 'disappeared' for the best part of a year in those days – but he had never confessed to my mother that he knew about her past in all of the thirty years that they'd been together. I imagine that he would have kept quiet because he didn't want to upset her. It is very sad to imagine how difficult it must have been for my mother to have carried her painful secret and her enormous grief alone for so long. My mother and all the rest of my family did eventually meet and get to know my half-brother. When my mother and he first met, he brought with him the little medal that she had placed on his tiny chest all those years before – a symbol of a mother's love. I was glad that she was able to know that he had a very happy childhood with his adoptive parents in Ireland, but sadly, once the lid had been taken off those three decades of contained grief, my mother's drinking escalated hugely.

The new insights that I gained during counselling allowed me to feel a little more compassion towards my mother, instead of the anger and disappointment which arose within me whenever I witnessed her destructive behaviour when she was drunk or when I felt very let down by her. I began to understand how, when I was a tiny baby, my mother's inability to bond closely would have caused me enormous stress and fear. As babies, we are helpless and entirely dependent on those closest to us for our survival. Any early connection that we develop, usually primarily to our mothers, but also to other caregivers, provides our very first imprint of how we sense the world. As babies, when someone holds us in a close embrace, we need to feel safe. We need also to sense that the person who holds us feels relaxed, and has time to focus entirely on us without being distracted or distressed. When gazing into the eyes of their caregivers, the child needs to see nothing but the look of love in those eyes, flooding their vulnerable little bodies with love so that they can feel secure and know that there is nothing to fear. When the child is hungry, they need to be able to trust that they will be fed, without resorting to crying in distress to get attention. I can't imagine how anyone can think that it is acceptable to advise parents that they should leave babies to cry and learn to settle themselves. Or that it will spoil the child if you keep picking them up and cuddling them every time they cry. I know that years ago this was normal practice – my mother once told me that she used to put me in the pram, wrapped up warmly, and leave me in the garden regardless of the weather for periods of time because it was widely believed that the fresh air was good for babies. Even now, there are some people who believe that babies shouldn't be fed on demand but instead be kept to a strict four-hourly feeding regime. It's no wonder that so many of us are riddled with insecurities.

I cannot know consciously what happened when my mother held me in her arms. Equally, I cannot know the degree of self-control I needed to be fully trained to use a potty by the age of thirteen months in order to please my parents –

my mother told me once that she hadn't wanted to have two babies in nappies at the same time, with my younger brother due just over a year after me. I can only imagine what my pre-verbal toddler self would have thought when I was sent away to stay with my aunt for a few weeks at the age of 14 months because my mum had just had another baby and didn't feel that she could cope with two babies immediately after having had a gall bladder operation. What I do know is that I would have experienced this separation from my mother and my father as a complete and terrifying abandonment, along with an innate sense of having done something dreadfully wrong, or been in some way completely unacceptable. A toddler believes that they are the centre of the universe, and the little girl who was me would have felt the utter terror and pain of rejection. I was told as an adult that during that time at my aunt's house I spent every day standing quietly looking out of the front room window, and being 'such a good girl'. Though apparently coping very well, in reality I would have been in deep shock. The impact of those early years will forever be imprinted deep within my subconscious.

One evening towards the end of my counselling course, I was doing a practice session with the tutor, but this time she was the counsellor and I was the client. She skilfully managed to bypass my usual defence mechanism of talking only about what I felt were safe subjects. I mentioned something about feeling angry towards Rob because I seemed to have to carry most of the responsibility for childcare, and the tutor steered the conversation around to my marriage, having astutely intuited that there was something else going on for me underneath the smokescreen issues around feeling guilty about being a working mum. I then brought up the subject of how guilty I felt about how I was rejecting Rob sexually. She asked me questions which I had never really allowed myself to ask.

"Do you love Rob?" she asked.

I was a bit taken aback by her straight to the point question.

I had to think about how to respond, because the answer didn't come automatically. After a pause, I said, "Er…no… I'm not sure…I don't think so…not any more. I don't think I'm in love with him…and it makes me feel guilty."

She then asked me, "Do you feel loved by him?" I thought for a few seconds and it dawned on me for the first time that, actually, I did not feel loved by him. I had been feeling guilty for all these years because I didn't love him enough, and now I wondered whether it wasn't just me who was unhappy in the marriage.

When I got home that evening, Rob was relaxing and watching television, lying on the sofa. I sat down in the chair opposite and quietly watched him for a short while. All of the things I wanted to say were compacted inside my chest like a concrete lump, but I was compelled to speak up and tell him how I felt.

I asked Rob if he ever wondered what I talked about in counselling.

"No, not really," he answered, whilst still looking at the television screen.

"I think it's a bit strange that you don't seem to even be interested," I said.

"Okay then, what do you talk about?" he said, turning towards me, using the TV remote to turn off the television with a dramatic flourish, making it clear that he was annoyed at my interrupting his viewing.

"I talk about how unhappy I feel."

"Unhappy about what?"

"About life in general, about you and me, about our marriage and how empty I feel."

"So, I might as well go now then, shall I?"

I paused, realising that here was an unexpected opportunity to be honest and brave enough to say something which I had never dared to say – something which might bring about a dramatic change to the shape of my entire life.

"Yes," I replied

There was silence for a few moments.

"Are you saying we should split up?" Rob asked.

My heart was thumping. I had spent years being so afraid of telling the truth about how I felt, and then, in one moment, there it was. Out on the table for discussion.

"Yes," I replied.

And so, it seemed that the decision to separate was made. As simple as that. I could hardly believe what had just transpired. Without saying anything else, I left Rob downstairs and quietly went upstairs to our bedroom. I slumped onto the bed and lay staring at the ceiling, absolutely still. I could hear my heart hammering, and the painful concrete lump in my chest had now extended into my throat as I thought about the bomb that we might be about to explode in the middle of the innocent little lives of our children.

After a few minutes, I got up from the bed and crept silently towards Evie and Daniel's bedroom. I gently opened their bedroom door. Evie and Daniel were both asleep – sprawled out like two starfish on top of their brightly coloured woodland animal duvets – snuffling in their sleep – two happy little four-year-olds. I sat on the chair between their beds and listened to their gentle snores, breathing in their familiar sweaty scent of fabric conditioner, shampoo and warm biscuits. I felt my heart constricting, a hard pain under my ribs and the beginning of tears as I looked at them. They had no idea how their world was going to implode.

I didn't know if I had the courage to do what I needed to do, because I knew that it would hurt my children so much. It would be absolutely contrary to my protective instincts as a mother to act so selfishly as to turn their lives upside down in order for me to be happy. However, there was a deep knowing within me, not quite fully tangible yet, but rooted in my own childhood experiences, that an angry and disconnected mother was actually probably more harmful to the emotional wellbeing of children than the effects of a parental split. I needed to trust this. Perhaps if I told myself that staying in a dead marriage would ultimately be harmful to my children, I could justify being prepared to end it. For years, I knew that I had at times been an angry and disconnected mother, sometimes struggling with the negative aspects of motherhood, yet believing that I had no right to feel anything other than positivity. I had been living for years mostly unaware that my teeth were clenched, though sometimes when I did become aware of it, I would consciously relax my lips to relieve the habitual rictus of my mouth. I used to drive around looking like a goldfish with my mouth wide open trying to relieve the tension in my jaw. I remember that my dentist could tell that I was grinding my teeth and he kept suggesting that I use a tooth guard at night.

I stroked Evie's and Daniel's hair in turn, very gently so that I didn't wake them. It was as though I was trying to soothe and calm them, but it was me who felt unsettled. After some time, I heard Rob coming up the stairs and, with some relief, I heard him going into the spare bedroom. I stayed in Evie and Daniel's bedroom for a long time, my heart raw with love just looking at them, before I finally crept back to my own bed.

9

Young Hearts Run Free
(Candi Staton 1976)

The next day, I awoke to the sound of Rob banging around downstairs in the kitchen. I could hear the twins playing in their bedroom, screeches of laughter interspersed with shrieks of frustration as they tussled over their toys. I looked at the clock on the bedside table – I still had some time before I needed to get up and ready for work, so I lay quietly waiting to hear the sound of Rob leaving the house. I didn't want to see him. I recalled our conversation from the night before and a wave of disbelieving shock reverberated deep in my stomach. Had we really agreed to separate? Had it really been so simple after all those years of feeling unhappy – yet too afraid to do anything about it? I wanted to stay there in the bed all morning and think about what had happened. Perhaps start to prepare myself for what I might say to Rob when he got home that evening. I heard the front door slam as Rob left for work and, sighing with a heavy heart, I rose slowly from my bed.

I looked at my reflection in the bathroom mirror and stared at myself for a few moments. I almost didn't recognise myself. My hair looked drab and nondescript, with outgrown blonde highlights leaving my mousy brown hair roots visible. I hadn't bothered going to the hairdressers for a very long time. What would have been the point? It seemed that nobody, including myself, was remotely interested in what I looked like. I was still slim, even after having a twin pregnancy. I used to like the way that I looked, but I couldn't see anything attractive about me as I looked in that mirror. I hadn't bothered to wear any make-up for as long as I could remember, even for work, which was something I would never have allowed to happen at one time. There was a deflated sadness emanating from my eyes. I attempted a pretend smile, feeling a bit ridiculous, but for a brief moment the silliness of it turned the fake smile into the beginnings of a real one, and I could see a tiny spark of my old self glinting in my eyes. I washed my face and found myself rooting through the bathroom cupboard, looking for my long disused make-up bag. There was an almost childlike frisson of excitement as I applied the cosmetics – as though I was a little girl playing dressing up – but afterwards I could see reflected back at me the hint of a genuine smile in my eyes, which minutes before had looked like a rather nondescript pale hazel, but with the accentuation of eye shadow and mascara really did look a little more of a rich brown colour and I looked a little more like the me that I remembered, the person I used to be.

I took a deep breath and tried to inject some lightness into my voice as I went in to Evie and Daniel to start the daily marathon of trying to get them washed, dressed and ready to go to the nursery so that I could go to work. I often referred to this time of day as 'World War Three'. Evie and Daniel never wanted to be with anyone but me or Rob, and would cry and struggle every time I needed to take them to childcare or nursery school. I couldn't rely on asking my parents to help with childcare, as I was concerned about whether my children might come to harm if my mother was under the influence of alcohol. As Rob's parents were already quite elderly, I didn't think it was right to expect them to be able to cope with looking after the twins for long periods when they were tiny babies, or two boisterous toddlers. The fact that neither of them drove meant that I couldn't ask them to help with taking the twins to nursery, or later to school, but they did become more involved with helping sometimes when the twins were a little older, as did my sister and my sister-in-law, with whom I sometimes had a reciprocal arrangement where we looked after each other's children from time to time. It was so exhausting having to do battle every day, like having to do a full day's work even before I went out of the door. Somehow, I had just accepted this as being normal life, and the somewhat unequal division of chores between us had never really fully registered with me. It seemed that Rob just had to get up, shower and have breakfast, then leave the house, as free as a bird, whereas I had to get myself ready, get the twins ready, put on a load of washing, plan the meal for the evening, and probably shop for it on the way home after work before I picked the children up, plus all the rest of it. When I got home from work, there was no time to relax before I started cooking the dinner whilst trying to play with Evie and Daniel, who would be vying for my attention, having not seen me since the morning. No wonder I was so tired. Why had I never really thought about this before? I'd just slipped into ways of being that really did not help me. Rob didn't behave as though he expected me to have his dinner on the table each night, but these patterns of behaviour had slowly evolved without us paying any attention to it.

World War Three was beginning to escalate as the twins started to assert their reluctance to get ready for nursery, and any pondering about my marriage was knocked into the long grass, as I was too busy to think, so I focussed on the task at hand and got the three of us on the road so that I wouldn't be late for work. Once the twins were secured in their car seats, I put on a sing-along CD and tried to cajole them into singing 'Ten Green Bottles' with me in order to distract them from whining about being taken to the nursery.

When Rob returned that evening, we awkwardly

performed our normal routine of putting Evie and Daniel to bed, and then we sat down to talk. It seemed that there was not much to say. Rob was clearly angry. We didn't discuss whether or not we should actually split up. Seeing Rob so upset triggered every guilt button that I possessed, but I could not bring myself to take a u-turn and suggest that we try to make things work between us. We did agree to try going for couples counselling with Relate, although I didn't believe by this point that our marriage was salvageable. I wondered if perhaps the counsellors might be able to help us to split up amicably. Rob and I decided that we would wait a few months until after Christmas for him to move out of the house, because we wanted to avoid creating sad memories for the twins which would make future Christmases forever painful for them by association.

The ensuing months living in the house together, knowing that we would be separating, and for a while hiding that knowledge from everyone, were very stressful. I did tell a couple of my very closest female friends about our decision to separate, and they were entirely supportive towards me. Rob and I gradually told our mutual friends and our immediate families. They mostly expressed surprise and sadness, but they seemed to understand without obviously judging us negatively. Rob and I circled cautiously around each other at home. Not saying very much, trying to put on a happy face for Evie and Daniel. I made an effort to be out when Rob was home, whenever possible, and he did the same with me. I felt terrible guilt about hurting him, and enormous fear about how the separation would affect our children. But underneath the fear was a distinct feeling of relief and at the edge of my awareness a sense of knowing that I was doing the right thing for all of us. If ever I had a wobble, I would remind myself that if I did not love Rob enough to remain married to him, then he would be better off with someone else who could love him wholeheartedly.

I did feel some sadness about the prospect of losing my relationship with Rob's parents when he and I separated. Evie and Daniel had become very close to them. One day I was alone with Rob's mother. By this time, she knew that we were planning to separate. I decided to try to broach the subject of our separation, and I started to tell her how sorry I felt for any hurt or distress that I was causing to everyone. I was so surprised when she calmly and kindly responded to me by telling me that she understood, and that she didn't judge me for my decision. She told me that she had always thought that Rob and I were in some ways incompatible, but that our separation wouldn't affect my relationship with her and her husband, and that they wanted to carry on seeing Evie, Daniel and myself as usual. This was borne out by that fact that we did remain very close and we saw each other frequently after the divorce, right up until the end of their long lives.

During the months before Rob and I separated, I started a new job as a Midwife Counsellor in the local maternity unit. My role was to support women who were emotionally distressed by adverse events related to pregnancy, ie stillbirth, miscarriage and fetal abnormalities. I managed the Early Pregnancy Assessment Clinic, and ran support groups for women experiencing infertility or pregnancy loss. Being distracted by my new job was good for me, and it helped me to focus to some extent on something other than the impending marital split. I didn't have to wear a uniform for my new job, and I found myself starting to find pleasure again in choosing nice clothes in bright colours to wear for work. I also began to wear a little make up every day, and treated myself by using nice perfume. I started to enjoy buzzing around the hospital, feeling the stirring of a new energy, and smiling at everyone I saw, whether I knew them or not. I realised that I was beginning to recapture a sense of my prior self as an outgoing and friendly person, a sense which I hadn't really experienced much since the beginning of the infertility process, apart from when I was pregnant with the twins. On some days, when I was feeling more positive, I even wore shorter skirts, instead of my usual drab midi skirts, showing off my long slim legs in my opaque black tights, feeling strength in my stride and a new liveliness bubbling within me as I strode happily around the hospital corridors. One of my Consultant colleagues used to laugh at me – always making comments on the length of my skirts – he used to say it must be a good day whenever I was wearing a mini-skirt! Although life at home whilst Rob was waiting to move out was still uncomfortable, there was a growing feeling of optimism within me. Even though I had no idea what my future might hold, and I knew that difficult times would be coming for us all, I didn't feel fear about becoming a single parent – just relief that I was in some way on the right track.

10

The First Time Ever I Saw Your Face
(Roberta Flack 1972)

Around a month after Rob and I decided to separate, something happened that was to change my life forever. I am always fascinated by the thought of how a person's life can be altered dramatically in a single heartbeat. How we can, in some ways, be just coasting through life, and then within just moments one tiny thing can occur, which may at the time not even be seen or considered significant, but which can be the starting point for something which will impact on your life in an enormous, as yet unseen, way. I consider the moment I first saw Ravi to be one of these moments.

From the very first time I set eyes upon Ravi, I was trying to get something from him which he either did not wish to give, or was unable to give to me, even if in that first moment, all I was trying to elicit from him was a smile. I did not know it then, but that one single moment was to foreshadow the dynamic of our relationship for the next thirteen years.

That prophetic event happened one morning whilst I was walking over to the medical records department to pick up the notes for the patients who were due to attend the Early Pregnancy Clinic. I say walking, but that day it was really more of a reluctant trudge, as I was trying to psyche myself up to face the utterly miserable clerk who manned the medical records reception. Every morning she would make me feel that I was making her life hell when I asked her to get the clinic notes for me. As if I was asking for something totally inappropriate, I would receive a stony look and one raised eyebrow when I gave her the list of patients for the clinic. Each time I would try to remain cheerful and polite, not expressing my anger and frustration with her unhelpfully obstructive attitude. No matter how nice I was to her, it never seemed to make any difference.

I was looking at the clinic list for that day as I walked over to the main hospital site, when I sensed that there was someone walking towards me. I lifted my head and saw the most beautiful man about to walk past me as I entered the main hospital corridor. I guessed that he might be Indian, extraordinarily handsome with soft brown eyes and one of those neat little moustaches worn typically by South Indian men. I remember noticing how smartly he was dressed, in his chinos and a crisp white doctor's coat. And for some reason I imagined how he would smell. Clean, fresh and masculine. I felt a little skip in my heartbeat.

I straightened up from my slightly downbeat posture, slowed down my walking pace, and looked straight at him. I offered him a smile, hoping for a smile in return, but he just looked at me with a very neutral facial expression. I swallowed a brief flush of embarrassment and continued walking without looking back, but I carried with me a new little fizz of excitement. I had an irrational feeling that I somehow recognised this good-looking stranger, although I knew that we had never met. Maybe he simply fitted some kind of subconscious physical blueprint for what I may have imagined would be my ideal man? I spent the next few weeks scanning the horizon for a sighting of him whenever I was at work. There seemed to be no sign of him.

As part of my job, I had to complete a return to midwifery course, which involved spending some time on the delivery suite.

"What are you doing here today?" Juliet, the midwife in charge of delivery suite asked me as I entered the labour ward office. There was no "hello" or "how are you?" I had known Juliet since I had been a student midwife and had never liked her abrupt and unfriendly manner. She shuffled around with a lazily lumbering gait, huffing and sighing as though she was dragging herself around reluctantly, maintaining a permanently pinched facial expression. I had always wondered how a person who seemed to be so lacking in warmth or communication skills ends up working in one of the caring professions. Now, more than forty years after the beginning of my nursing career, I know that even the nicest of people can become toughened and hard-faced as a result of constant stress, so I do not judge so quickly. You may, by now, already be guessing that I have a preternatural level of discomfort when I am in the presence of a person who is not smiling.

"Yes…I think I am supposed to be working with you today if that's okay?" I replied, trying to force my facial expression into some semblance of a friendly smile.

Juliet sighed. "I suppose it will have to be, won't it? Not a great day for having a student hanging around me, I have to say," she mumbled as she turned her back to me.

"Sorry…I'm not a student – I'm a midwife – and I'm doing a return to midwifery course. I'll try not to bother you too much!" I said, with a forced laugh, attempting to inject a little fake humour into our interaction through my clenched teeth, and trying to pretend that I felt unaffected by Juliet's rudeness and hostility towards me. I felt very unwelcome in the delivery suite that day.

I always find it uncomfortable to be in the position of the new learner who is not yet competent, having left a job where I have been skilled and known exactly what I was doing. However, if you were to look at my very long curriculum vitae and observe my notable history of being very much a job hopper, you might assume that, despite my discomfort with being seen as incompetent, I seem to have some kind of compulsion to put myself in the position of the perpetual novice over and over again. This tendency of mine to change jobs frequently, particularly when something wasn't right in my life, was to become a pattern throughout my nursing career. It is only in retrospect that I can understand some of the reasons for this – they have become clearer to me now that I am no longer a nurse.

"We're just waiting for the anaesthetist for room 5," Juliet said.

There was nowhere to sit in the hot and crowded delivery suite office. Midwives and healthcare assistants bustled in and out. The air was filled with the noise of chatter, telephones ringing, and I could hear the intrusive and repetitive buzzing of the patients' call bells.

I decided not to attempt any further conversation with Juliet, so I foraged through the medical records trolley until I found the notes folder for the patient in room 5. I took the notes into the corridor and continued to read them as I leaned against the wall in the corridor outside the office in the relative quiet. I took them back into the office and sat down on the only available chair.

"Hi Dr Pathappan! Are you doing the epidural?" I heard Juliet say, and I sensed by the tone of her voice that her usually sullen demeanour had been apparently transformed. I looked up to see who she was talking to and I saw that it was the beautiful Indian doctor I had seen a few weeks previously.

As I listened to Juliet telling the doctor about the patient, I sat up on the edge of my chair – suddenly on high alert. The sound of the doctor's voice and his soft Indian accent triggered a feeling of physical pleasure in my lower abdomen. I realised that he was the anaesthetist who would be administering the epidural for the patient, so I looked at the information board to see who was on call for anaesthetics.

Ravi Pathappan – so, that's his name! I thought.

I followed Ravi and Juliet into the corridor, and then into the patient's room on the delivery suite. Juliet had adopted a calmly professional manner, but I noticed a tiny glint in her eyes as she talked to Ravi. I felt a stab of jealousy as I realised that she was flirting with him. *Don't be ridiculous – I don't even know him,* I thought to myself. But the feeling was there nonetheless. Already I was possessive.

I listened as Ravi explained to the patient and her husband what would happen when he administered the epidural. I was transfixed by Ravi's voice – the gentle sing-song lilt of his Malayalam accent. Whilst Juliet began to help the patient to get into position for the epidural to be inserted, I started preparing the equipment trolley for the procedure.

Ravi turned towards the trolley and started to open a package of surgical gloves. I watched his hands as he opened up more of the packages of sterile equipment. I noticed his slender fingers. Neat and clean finger nails. His hands were beautiful. I was standing close enough to be able to smell him – a mixture of aftershave, pleasantly musky sweat and the disinfectant odour of hospital which clings to the clothing of hospital workers. I was conscious that my hands were trembling. I could feel my heart racing and a flush of heat was rising from my neck into my face and ears. I seemed to be somehow affected physically by Ravi's close proximity to me. I was like a silly love-struck schoolgirl. As I tried to open the sterile packages onto the procedure trolley, I was clumsy and fumbling. I ripped them open messily and managed to drop a pack of gauze swabs on the floor. My face blushed – a deep shade of red.

"Oh…I'm sorry," I said to Ravi, stumbling on my words as my mouth was so dry.

"No problem," he replied. And again, I was transfixed by his voice, triggering something inside me.

I tried to focus on controlling my breath and on the task of assisting him with the procedure. Ravi remained quietly focussed and the epidural was completed quickly and efficiently. He left the room, giving a brief smile to the couple and telling them that he hoped all would go well for them.

Juliet left the room, saying "I'll be back in a minute" and I sat down on a chair beside the bed. I wanted to leave the room and follow Ravi, but I took a deep breath and switched decisively into professional mode, then started to chat with the patient and her husband.

11

It's In His Kiss

(Betty Everett 1964)

A couple of weeks later, I was at the hospital social club one evening with one of my midwife friends, Nicole. We were sitting with a couple of other male friends who were going to play badminton in the court next door. The plan was that they would join Nicole and me again for another drink once they had finished their game.

I heard the entrance door to the social club open, so I looked up and saw Ravi walking in, holding a badminton racquet. My heart skipped a beat. I realised that he must be going to join our friends to play badminton. I pointed Ravi out to Nicole.

"There's Dr Pathappan – the guy I was telling you about!" I said, looking towards the door. "Isn't he beautiful?"

"Yes, I can see what you mean!" Nicole giggled.

We spent the next hour with my gaze fixed on the door to the badminton court. Eventually, it opened and our friends, accompanied by Ravi, came over to join us. I somehow discreetly managed to engineer it so that I was sitting next to Ravi. I was unable to believe this stroke of luck. I joined in with the conversation as it roamed around the group, but my attention was fixed on Ravi.

"I've seen you around maternity," Ravi said, turning towards me.

"Yes, I work there. I am a Midwifery and Gynaecology Counsellor. I run the Early Pregnancy clinic," I said.

He noticed me! I thought.

I wanted to stare at him but tried to avert my eyes as we spoke.

"Where are you from?" I asked

"India," he said.

"I've always wanted to go to India. It's the spiritual side of it all which interests me," I said.

Then I started to gabble nervously.

"I wish I'd have gone there years ago, but I got married young. I've got two young children now, so it will be a long time until I will be able to go to India."

I shared with him that I had a long held, but rather vague, notion, that, when my children were grown up and independent, I would run off to India and do some kind of voluntary work – perhaps in HIV/ AIDS. I suppose subconsciously I was trying to give him the message that I was unhappily married. I thought I may not get the chance to speak to him again and I wanted to make a connection.

Intermittently, Ravi and I re-joined the group conversations, but I wanted to talk only with him. I felt uncharacteristically shy and I didn't know what else to say.

After a while, Ravi turned towards me again.

"Have you heard of a book called the Tao of Physics?" he asked, and when I said that I hadn't, he proceeded to tell me about the opening paragraph of the book which alludes to theories of quantum physics, describing how the ocean is just pure energy. All of those atoms in a beautiful dance with all of the other elements of creation.

I was excited, as I imagined from his comments that he must be very interested in spiritual perspectives if he read such books. I continued to avert my gaze from him and picked up my drink. I sat quietly, waiting to see what he might say next. I was concentrating on trying to stop my hands shaking as I nursed my vodka and coke.

And then, the most amazing thing happened.

"Have you ever thought about how, in the ocean, there are millions and millions of little waves, moving and rolling, forever changing...and then, sometimes, two of these tiny waves will meet and combine to make a huge wave?" Ravi asked me.

I felt a sudden rush of intense physical pleasure pulsating through my whole body – an incredible surge of tingling heat running through me from the top of my head to the tips of my toes. My face flushed and my heart was thumping. I couldn't look at Ravi. I momentarily stopped breathing. I tried to suppress my physical reaction to him because I was concerned that everyone else around the table might be able to sense what was going on between us. It was like having an orgasm in public and trying not to show it. I knew in this moment that Ravi was referring to him and me. We were the little waves who had just collided and created a huge wave – a tsunami. I knew that whatever was happening for me, he was feeling something too. I had to remind myself to keep breathing.

By the end of the evening Ravi and I had decided to meet up somewhere on our own to chat. The decision was made with one question from him and a yes from me. We didn't talk about the fact that what we were planning to do in secret was perhaps wrong and deceptive, as Rob hadn't yet moved out. We couldn't let ourselves look at this aspect, but I knew that I had to see him, no matter what.

On our first date, I picked Ravi up from the hospital and we drove out to a country pub where nobody would see us. I couldn't believe I was actually in the car alone with him. This man to whom I had been so immediately attracted from the first moment I saw him. We bought our drinks and went to sit in the pub garden. We sat astride a picnic bench facing each other. We were like a pair of awkward teenagers. We hadn't yet found our rhythm in conversation, stopping and starting with spurts of inane nonsense, and then laughing as we both kept starting to speak at the same time. I had written a poem about the moment when Ravi talked about waves and we had both acknowledged the connection and energy between us in the hospital social club. I took the poem out of my pocket.

"You'll probably think I'm really weird, but I wrote this poem," I said as I handed the poem to him. "I wanted to capture that wonderful moment in the social club when I knew that you were feeling something too."

Ravi read the poem and looked at me. He said nothing, but slid along the bench towards me and put his arms around me. We sat like that for some time in an embrace. His cheek felt warm against my face and I could smell the clean citrus woody scent of him. He slowly moved his face so that his lips brushed against mine and we shared the gentlest of kisses – as soft as the brush of a butterfly's wings. I could hardly breathe with excitement.

Soon after this meeting in the pub garden, Ravi left his job at the hospital and started a new job at a hospital almost eighty miles away. I had not seen him since our kiss on the pub bench. Ravi didn't phone me as I was still living with Rob, although I was able to phone him from time to time at the doctors' residence at the hospital. This was in the days before we had mobile phones. I had told Ravi that Rob and I had already decided to split up and that we were waiting until after Christmas so that we wouldn't ruin Christmas for

Evie and Daniel. I was desperate to go to see Ravi, but he was reluctant to see me as he felt very uncomfortable about the fact that I was still married. Despite my reassurances to the contrary, Ravi was extremely anxious not to be implicated as being in any way responsible for the breakdown of my marriage.

Christmas was now looming. At home, Rob and I were going through the motions of parenting and working, and we had fixed a date for him to move out after Christmas once we had told the children about the breakup of our marriage and given them a little time to absorb the reality of this prospect, as much as they were able to at such a young age. Although the dynamics between Rob and me were very uncomfortable, I was now nurturing a solid feeling of enormous hope and wonder about Ravi, which sustained me with huge positivity about what the future might hold. I was floating on an undercurrent of excitement, as I trusted that when the time was right, I would be able to see Ravi and we would no longer have to hide our relationship. Rob and I had agreed that he would move in with a friend of his temporarily, and then I would find somewhere to rent for me and the twins. The plan was for Rob to return to the house once I had moved out. I did go to a solicitor prior to the separation, but unfortunately, I received some very poor advice which was to have a hugely detrimental impact on my future financial security. I felt that there was no way that I could afford to buy Rob out and keep the mortgage going as a single parent working part-time. We had a large mortgage and very little equity in our home, so we agreed that Rob would buy me out of the mortgage with a very small amount of money and I would start again by myself, using this bit of money to furnish a rented property. I didn't speak to my family or friends about our plans regarding a financial settlement. It didn't occur to me to try to find out whether I might be able to claim any kind of housing benefit which might have helped me to stay in my home. I think that I believed that I was responsible for the decision to have children and then split up, so maybe I had no right to expect the state to pay towards a roof over my head. I felt overwhelmingly guilty about ending our marriage, and Rob was extremely angry with me. As an inveterate people pleaser, I couldn't bear his anger towards me. We had immediately adopted the roles of perpetrator and victim, with Rob being the victim. I know now that it takes two people to make a marriage not work, and it takes enormous courage to be the one brave enough to call time on a dead relationship, but at the time I was so anxious about placating Rob that I agreed to this rather unfair deal. I only began to realise in retrospect how I had made myself and my children very vulnerable.

Christmas passed and the day came for Rob and me to tell the children about what was going to happen. It was an experience I will never forget. It was incredibly painful for all of us. Rob and I spoke gently, taking turns to speak. We tried to reassure Evie and Daniel that we loved them and that it was not in any way their fault that we were going to split up. We told them that they would live with me but would still see their dad very often. Daniel reacted by going very quiet, moving away from me and refusing to let me put my arms around him. I felt the floor disappear from under my feet at his rejection of me in that awful moment. Evie started to cry immediately, and threw herself onto the lowest step of the stairs with a gut-wrenching howl. She was utterly distraught, and I felt sick with guilt for inflicting this terrible emotional pain on them both. As I looked at my little children, just four years old at the time, and at Rob, I felt ashamed of myself and shocked at my own selfishness.

As a mother, it is instinctual to put our children's needs, and usually anybody else's needs, before one's own. Mothers are often driven to please others – we are expected to fit in with the societal archetype of the selfless giver of love and succour – the nurturer. A lot of the time we are not even aware of what our own needs are, let alone able to ensure those needs are met. I think though that for me this was the first time in my life that I was able to know very clearly what I actually did feel, and able to act upon that. I did not know how we were all going to get through this process of marital separation, but I did know deep in my soul that I could not stay in this unhappy marriage.

12

Oh, What A Night

(The Dells 1959)

The day came for Rob to leave, and I remember standing at the front door with Evie and Daniel, watching Rob walk up the garden path carrying some of his belongings. The twins were crying, and my heart was pounding with fear and guilt. After Rob had driven away, I spent the rest of the day trying to soothe Evie and Daniel with constant cuddles and by distraction with nice food treats and quiet games. Somehow, we got through the day and then at an earlier than usual bed time, the twins and I slept in my bed, huddled together and exhausted from emotional distress.

Gradually, we all began to adapt to our new life. At first, Evie and Daniel were frequently upset and tearful, saying that they missed their dad, and my heart would sink with guilt every time they said it. But in time they learned to accept that even though their father was not now living in the same house, they could still see him often. The bouts of crying began to lessen, and they got used to spending alternate Friday nights at Rob's new place, but were often reluctant to be apart from me. They seemed to be experiencing a lot of anxiety when they started going to their new primary school – I thought that their reaction to this change, and their ability to cope with it, was worse than I might have expected. Again, I felt wracked with guilt – berating myself for causing Evie and Daniel to lose confidence in themselves. They had lost their sense of security in the world because of me and I didn't know how to make it better. One day, I gave them a little rose quartz crystal heart each and suggested that they could put them in their school uniform pockets. I said that if they had moments at school when they felt anxious or upset, they could hold the crystal heart in the palm of their hands and it would remind them that I loved them very much. It did seem to help them both a little as a small anchor of positivity.

Eventually, I started to feel a little calmer, realising that although I was now a single parent, my daily routine with looking after Evie and Daniel and working part time at the maternity unit was essentially unchanged. It had always been me who'd had to sort out childcare anyway, nearly always been me rather than Rob who'd had to take time off work if the children were unwell, so there was nothing different about that now. Despite all the upset, I felt sure that I had done the right thing, and there was an increasingly tangible sense of relief for me which underpinned everything.

I now had every other Friday night free as the twins were with Rob. Finally, I was able to arrange to see Ravi. We decided that I would go to see him in his flat near the hospital where he worked, so we arranged the date for this. The day came, and that evening, after Rob had picked up Evie and Daniel, I began to prepare myself, using scented bath oils and putting on some sexy new lingerie which I'd bought recently, especially for this occasion. I stood in front of the mirror and inspected myself closely. It had been a long time since anyone but me had seen my body, and although I was feeling very excited at the prospect of possibly making love with Ravi that night, I did feel anxious about him seeing me naked. I was still slim, but my abdomen was soft and doughy, covered in fine silvery stretch marks from my twin pregnancy. Prior to having my twins, I'd always had quite a flat chest, but now my breasts were slightly larger, and I enjoyed seeing that I had a little hint of cleavage in my under-wired bra. I reassured myself that I looked good enough.

The Friday evening rush hour traffic was slow on my journey to Ravi's. I was so anxious to reach my destination and to see Ravi, that I became quite agitated every time the queue on the M25 ground to a halt. Listening to the radio didn't help to distract me. I just needed to get there.

After a couple of frustrating hours in the stop-start traffic, I arrived at Ravi's flat. As soon as I saw him, I put my arms around him and hugged him tightly. He laughed a little nervously at my overt display of affection. We sat on his sofa and he asked me if I wanted a drink. I declined, and then I took his hand and stood up, and said, quite uncharacteristically brazenly, "No, I want to go to bed with you."

Again, Ravi laughed nervously, and I really couldn't quite believe how forward I was being. All I knew in that moment was that I wanted him with a ravenous desire like nothing I had ever experienced. I had spent years feeling shut down in my body. I had been dead inside, with no sexual desire. Now I felt incredibly alive. I was bursting with fire and energy. Very soon we were naked. We did not have time for foreplay. I wanted him inside me. I had brought condoms with me, although I was protected for contraception as I had started taking the pill again in preparation for this new relationship. I was aware of the risks of contracting a sexually transmitted infection with a new partner – after all, I had previously worked for a while as a sexual health nurse. When the time came and I knew that he was about to penetrate me, I thought briefly about the packet of condoms which I'd placed in readiness on the bedside table. I didn't want to use them. I wanted to feel him inside me. I wanted no barriers between his body and mine. I wanted to feel his fluid inside me and take a part of him away with me when I left him. There were a few seconds where I allowed some rational thoughts to enter my consciousness, asking myself, *What if I catch HIV? What about my children if I caught HIV and died?*

And recklessly, I remember thinking in that moment, *If I die, I die. It will be worth it.*

And so, we didn't use any condoms. We made love repeatedly that night and the next morning. I had brought some little tea lights to create a warm and romantic light, (and reduce the risk of illuminating my stretchmarks!) and I placed them on top of a wooden cabinet in the room. By the time we finished, the candles had long burned out and left three circular burn marks on the wood.

As I drove home the next day, I felt as though my body was almost vibrating with a warm glow of intense happiness and pleasure, and I started to reflect on what had happened. I knew for sure that I was in love with Ravi and that I wanted to be with him for the rest of my life. Even though we hardly knew each other, I felt that I had been waiting for the whole of my life to meet him. I know this all sounds a bit like a Mills and Boon cliché, but it is truly how I felt. The madness of falling in love carries universal themes, although when it is happening to us, we really do believe that nobody has ever felt this way before.

In the rational light of the following day, I found it hard to credit my dismissive thoughts about the risks of unprotected sex whilst I had been in the throes of intense sexual arousal the previous night. My rational self would never consider it to be acceptable to take such a chance on something which might be so harmful to me, or indeed ultimately to my children. To think that in those moments I had believed that to experience the pleasure of sex without a condom was more important than my life, seemed to be utterly ridiculous. It taught me a huge lesson which was to influence my work as a sexual health nurse in the future. I understood then, from personal experience, how even the most well informed and cautious person could make unwise and risky decisions when in the heat of passion, and do things which they may never have considered themselves capable of doing. So, in the years ahead as a nurse, whenever I was counselling patients who had in some way made a harmful decision for themselves regarding sexual behaviour, maybe contracted a sexually transmitted infection by having unprotected sex with a new partner, or become pregnant due to not using contraception, or had sex with someone other than their partner, I was able to understand, in a very visceral and personal way, the power of intense sexual arousal to cloud our personal judgement and decision-making processes.

13

Midnight At the Oasis

(Maria Muldaur 1974)

A pattern started to emerge where I would spend each day for a fortnight in a state of excited anticipation of alternate Friday nights. During the weeks, I was managing life as a single parent quite easily, although already finances were becoming a bit of a tighter struggle on my part-time salary. I had made a conscious decision to continue working part-time even though I couldn't really afford to. I wanted to be able to pick Evie and Daniel up from school as much as possible. I wanted them to feel connected to me as a mother and I didn't want to have to rely too much on childcare. I reasoned that if I built up debts, I could always repay them once the twins had grown up, as then I would be able to work for longer hours. I knew that I would never be able to reclaim their time as children.

Evie and Daniel were settling into our new routine, and they seemed happier. I was still working part-time in my job in the maternity unit, so I was able to pick the twins up from school each day. We had plenty of time to do fun things together, such as play dates and sleepovers with friends, and I was able to wholly engage myself with cooking nice dinners for the three of us, with lovely relaxing evenings playing with Evie and Daniel before we settled down to reading together at bedtime. I felt calm and happy, able to be the relaxed, patient and kind mother that I had always wanted to be. There was an unfamiliar sense that some kind of vague underlying rage, or an unspecific fear, had been lifted from me.

When the eagerly awaited Friday evenings arrived, I would set off through the rush hour traffic on the long motorway journey to Ravi's. As soon as I arrived, we would get straight into bed and then stay there, sometimes not even bothering to eat. On the Saturday evening, I would reluctantly prise myself out of the bed, before travelling home, exhausted but elated, just in time before Rob brought Evie and Daniel home. I felt incredibly happy. I was completely in love and I felt confidently full of hope for the future. Each time I saw Ravi I felt as though I had come home to a place where I had always been destined to be. I was fascinated by every aspect of him. I adored the smell of him. In my bedside drawers I kept an empty bottle of the after shave which he wore, and an old bottle of his shower gel, so that I could remind myself of his smell when I wasn't with him. I adored his beautiful light brown skin and soft black body hair, and I was thrilled by the contrast of his body with my own pale skin and blonde hair. I would stare at his face, whether he was asleep or awake, utterly besotted by every line of it. Whenever I was near to him my heart would beat a little faster. I had undergone a complete metamorphosis – no longer a stone-cold statue, I was now a hot-blooded wild woman, pulsating with love and desire. Ravi seemed to adore my body, and he too was hungry for the physical connection between us. The two of us were drowning in desire. I felt like a goddess being worshipped by him. Ravi sometimes called me Aphrodite. I had never before felt so in touch with my own body and with my capacity to give and receive sexual pleasure. It was absolutely intoxicating. I certainly didn't feel as though I had a psychosexual problem in those wildly erotic times.

I have always held a fascination for anything Indian, so I would be enthralled as I listened to Ravi tell me about life in India. He sometimes played a CD of beautiful classical Indian music when we made love, and in my mind I was transported to another world. Ravi gave me little gift items from India, the first of which was a very small elephant carved from stone which had a tiny baby elephant carved inside it. I treasured this elephant and would carry it with me in my pocket, like a holy relic, thinking of Ravi every time I felt the coolness of the stone in my palm, and then I would place it on my bedside table each night so that I could see it before I went to sleep and as soon as I woke each morning. Although Ravi worked as a doctor, he was also a very talented artist. He was always quite self-effacing about his art. I was astounded to see some of his beautiful paintings. Ravi had been reluctantly pushed into a medical career by his parents, both of whom were doctors, as were his brother and sister. Ravi's family were all in India, and Ravi had left to work as a doctor in England after completing his medical training in India. I gradually learned that there was a cultural and family expectation that, as the eldest son, Ravi would marry a suitable Indian girl and return to live in the family home in India, so that he could fulfil his responsibility of looking after his parents as they aged. I could see that I, as a divorced, English mother of two, didn't quite fit into this future picture, but I was so sure of my love for Ravi and of his love for me that I believed we would find some way of working things out.

Those first few months really were magical. Ravi and I gradually progressed to leaving the bed occasionally to venture out for dinner together, or to spend days in London exploring art in various museums, getting pleasantly inebriated and giggling together in cosy pub corners. We were learning to adjust to each other's cultural differences. I was always physically demonstrative and would try to hold Ravi's hand when we walked together in public, but Ravi initially found this very strange, as this would have been seen as inappropriate in his native India. He told me that it wasn't usual for couples even to dance together in public – in India he had only seen dance being performed on a stage. So, when Ravi initially held his arms stiffly by his sides as we walked together, I would prise his arms open so that I could link my arms with his and gently tease him about being in what I called his 'Irish dancing mode'! Ravi wanted to teach me how to paint, so he and I started painting a picture together. He was helping me to learn how to see colours differently, to notice the visual world around me in a new way.

I soon began to realise that Ravi was not an emotionally demonstrative man and that he didn't seem to have a wide circle of friends, but this just made me feel privileged – somehow special – to be the one person he allowed to get close to him. It seemed to me that Ravi mostly spent his days either at work or in his flat sleeping and recovering from his exhausting and stressful work as an anaesthetist. Very occasionally he would tell me that he was meeting up with one of his male work colleagues for a drink, and I knew that he was in contact with one very close friend who worked as a doctor in Belgium, but other than that he didn't seem to have much of a social life. Whenever Ravi and I were together, it was always just the two of us. For a long time, we didn't seem to need the company of anyone else as we only had eyes for each other, but I was so full of love that after a while I was bursting with it – desperate to tell everyone about this beautiful man with whom I was so besotted. I wanted my children, my family and my friends to meet Ravi. And this is where the problems first began to emerge.

It began to dawn on me that, although I was curious about Ravi's life before he met me and I wanted to know all about his friends and his family, my curiosity didn't seem to be reciprocated. I felt very proud to be with him and I wanted him to tell me that he felt the same about me. I felt loved by him, but I wanted him to tell me that he loved me. I had already intuited that Ravi didn't find it easy to talk openly about anything emotional. I had learned that there was a risk of ruining the mood whenever I tried to start a gently probing conversation about feelings, so I chose my moment carefully when I asked him how he felt about me. Ravi replied, "Whenever I've met women before, I would always think they were an oasis at first, but then each one turned out to be a mirage. I wondered if it would be the same with you, but you are actually the oasis." I took this as Ravi's way of telling me that his love for me was different to anything he had experienced before, and that it was real.

14

Butterfly

(Mariah Carey 1997)

After the endorphin-induced blindness of the first few months of our relationship, I gradually became conscious of the uncomfortable tension in living two different lives. I had one life as a mother to Evie and Daniel, and the other as a lover to Ravi. When I was with Ravi at the weekends, I missed my children, and I was in a constant state of anxiety about being away from them. There were no mobile phones at this time in the nineties, but I did manage to buy an electronic pager so that at least I could be contacted in an emergency when I was away from home. I felt continuously guilty about being so far away from home should an emergency happen. On weekdays, even though I was enjoying being a much more relaxed mother with Evie and Daniel, my body and soul ached with missing Ravi. I thought that the time was right for him to meet my children, for me to integrate my two lives into one, so I asked him if he would come to my house one weekend. Ravi refused, saying that he didn't feel comfortable about coming to the house that had been my marital home. I very quickly realised that even though I was now separated from Rob, and I knew that Rob had by this time happily found a new partner, Ravi still didn't want me to tell anyone about our relationship. I couldn't really understand why. So, apart from my two very close friends who knew about Ravi, both of whom were pleased for me to have found new love, I reluctantly respected Ravi's wishes and continued to keep my new relationship a secret from almost everybody, including Evie and Daniel. Ravi and I carried on seeing each other on alternate Friday nights at his place. We still didn't socialise with anyone else. From time to time, I would raise the issue about his need to remain hidden in my life and his apparent need to keep me hidden in his. I began to feel as though I was a shameful secret. When I questioned Ravi and tried to persuade him to open up to our friends and family about our relationship, he seemed to indicate that his reticence was entirely due to the fact that he felt uncomfortable as a result of his cultural background. He told me that he knew his family would never be able to accept his being with me. My children and I would be a source of embarrassment and shame. Ravi would sometimes say that he wished that we had met many years before, when we were younger, meaning, I suppose, before I'd married Rob and become a mother. Whilst I could understand this sentiment, I didn't like the fact that the very existence of my children seemed to be considered by Ravi to be a source of regret.

Although I was still totally besotted with Ravi, my discomfort about his inability to accept the reality that I was a mother began to create uncomfortable undercurrents between us. Each time I tried to bring up the subject, I felt like I was nagging and making Ravi angry, and he would stall me with his silence. So, I'd shut down, then the conversation would falter and we would get nowhere. I started to write long letters outlining all of my thoughts and feelings, and I would leave these letters for him to read after I'd left him on a Saturday evening. He used to dread receiving these 'ten sides of A4', as he called them. I still have copies of these letters, and they make for very sad reading. They show so clearly how much I loved him and how I was trying so desperately, almost pleading with Ravi to make some kind of long-term commitment to me.

On one occasion, Ravi told me that he thought of happiness as being like a butterfly landing on the palm of your hand, and that all you should do is let your hand remain open and enjoy the beauty of the butterfly for as long as it wants to stay there. He said that if the butterfly chooses to fly away then let it fly, and if you try to capture the butterfly by closing your fingers around it, you will damage the butterfly. I responded to this imagery by somehow managing, as a non-artist, to create a fairly good oil pastel painting of a hand with a blue butterfly on the open palm, which I gave as a gift to Ravi. I was always trying to show how much I loved him – and working hard, it seems, to earn his love, to please him.

Although Ravi wasn't responding to me in the way that I wanted him to, there was something quite fascinating to me about his spiritual way of thinking and his use of metaphorical imagery. I understood that the butterfly represented Ravi – not in the sense that Ravi was fluttering around lightly and freely in the world, but rather that he seemed to feel that he might become trapped in some way if he made any commitment to me. I presented the metaphor of myself as the oasis back to him, saying that he was just walking fearfully around the water's edge, dipping a toe into the water, but that if he was to 'immerse himself in the water', ie: to commit wholeheartedly to our relationship, he might find that the water felt wonderfully warm and would actually support him rather than drown him.

There seemed to be a deep sadness in Ravi, something held-back and fearful that prevented him from fully engaging in life. He was unhappy in his work as an anaesthetist, having been forced into medicine by his parents. I used to wonder if he, as a quiet and introverted man, had chosen to become an anaesthetist thinking that he wouldn't have to talk much with patients as they were all asleep? Unfortunately for him, the increasing use of local and spinal anaesthetics meant that he often did have to converse with his patients more than he might have expected. Ravi sometimes said that he wished that he could leave medicine completely and have a new career doing something creative. Even though I had little money, I offered to support him if he wanted to give up his job as an anaesthetist and undertake a new degree. I told him that he could come and live with me and the twins and he wouldn't have to pay rent, since I was already just about meeting the household expenses. I just wanted him to be happy. Ravi chose not to accept my offer.

As much as I loved Ravi, I was becoming increasingly upset at his unwillingness to engage fully in our relationship. I was tired of always having to drive to him at the weekends – apart from the fact that I couldn't really afford the petrol. I was exhausted with living a double life. I wanted to do normal things together as a couple and with Evie and Daniel. I wanted us to be a family. I missed Ravi when I wasn't with him and I wished that we could see each other every day, to eat dinner together each evening and to snuggle up in bed together every night. Like a normal couple. By now, I had moved out of the home I shared with Rob so that he could move back in, and I had made a nice little home for myself and the twins in a pleasant rented flat. I had imagined that our tenancy in the flat would not be for the long term, as I believed that at some point Ravi and I might live together. Ravi and I did sometimes talk about this as a theoretical possibility – something which would happen at some point in the future when he was ready. I was hoping that Ravi would consider buying a house with me near to where I was living at the time, but I was prepared, if necessary, to move to be near to his work and re-locate my job and the twins' schooling, although I did sometimes wonder if Ravi might be stalling until my children had grown up and left home. While I was waiting for Ravi to make a decision about me, I felt that I was living in limbo and couldn't move forward with trying to find a proper permanent home for the twins and myself, as I didn't want to uproot them any more than was necessary, especially after the upheaval of the divorce. Whenever I tried to encourage Ravi to move forward in our relationship, he always gave me the impression that he would do so when the time was right. There was always something else in his life which he needed to sort out first, for example: his parents in India, or an exam related to his work, and then he would be able to think clearly about us. His stock answer was always 'I'm not ready yet', so I extrapolated from the use of the word 'yet' that he would be ready at some point, if only I was patient enough to wait. I felt that he loved me, and I did understand the reality of the cultural differences which would need to be overcome, so most of the time I tried to accept that I had to wait. Sometimes however, my patience would wear thin and I would send him another one of my ten sides of A4 telling him that I didn't want to be with him anymore and that he should go and find himself a little Indian virgin. We would stay apart for a couple of weeks, I would ache with missing him, trying to resist the urge to contact him, but at the same time being almost afraid to take a bath or shower in case he might phone and I wouldn't be able to answer. Eventually, he would always phone me – and the pleasure and relief of hearing his voice on the phone would be akin to the rush of an addict mainlining heroin. Each time we reunited I felt a huge surge of joy and relief. Neither of us wanted to be with anyone else. It was emotionally exhausting, but the drama of it felt intense – and I imagine the repeated dopamine hit of relief and pleasure each time we reconciled was probably quite addictive.

It would actually be two more years of our cycling through breakups and reconciliations before he agreed to meet Evie and Daniel, who were by now six years old. And as I write this, I am seeing the awful reality of that as if for the first time. How on earth could I have thought that it was in any way acceptable for him to so wholly discount the reality of me as a mother? Equally, how could it have been in any way acceptable that I allowed myself to continue in the relationship despite this? It would be many years before I could even begin to understand why I was so prepared to discount my own needs in order to meet Ravi's needs – how I was able to abandon myself so completely – but unfortunately, I did not arrive at this awareness before events were to occur as a result of my need to please him, which would absolutely derail me.

15

You Can't Hurry Love

(The Supremes 1966)

Ravi's relationship with my children was tentative. He always spoke kindly to Evie and Daniel, although he seemed shy around them, and I knew that he didn't actively want to spend time with them or get to know them. We did try to do occasional activities together with the twins, just day trips to fairly local places, but they were few and far between, and often a bit uncomfortable for all of us. We never had an actual holiday together. There were some sweet little gestures from Ravi towards the children – he used to amuse Evie and Daniel by doing magic tricks, and on their birthdays, he would give them money – crisp bank notes that he had actually ironed so that they looked nicer. Ravi was always more relaxed when he and I were alone, and my children were happier when they had me to themselves. I was torn between them and wished so much that I could find a way of bridging the gap between my two lives. I tried to explore with Ravi about his feelings now.

"Ravi, having met Evie and Daniel, has it made you feel any clearer about whether you think you could live with us?" I asked.

"They are nice children, but I don't want to be a father to someone else's children," Ravi replied.

"But you wouldn't be their father. They already have a father. You would be their stepfather – and you wouldn't be responsible for them financially – that's mine and Rob's responsibility."

"Yes, but what if when they are teenagers, they tell me to fuck off because I'm not their dad?" Ravi asked.

"Well, I suppose it's possible that they might say that, but you would need to be adult enough to deal with it", I replied.

I decided to let the subject rest, to be patient and just appreciate that there was some small shift, in that he had at last met Evie and Daniel and we were no longer keeping our relationship secret from my family and friends. Even though glacial in its speed, I had to acknowledge that this was at least a little bit of progress towards the future together that I dreamed of.

For a while, Ravi and I settled into a happier period of alternating between me travelling to him when the children were with Rob, or Ravi coming to stay with me and the twins at the weekends. I started to introduce Ravi to some of my friends and family. He always seemed like a quieter version of himself when we were with others, but everyone seemed to like and accept him, apart from my friend Annabelle who, having met him once just briefly and having listened to me for years talking about my issues in the relationship, wisely and intuitively advised me that she believed that one day I would need Ravi to be strong enough to make a serious decision and that he wouldn't be capable of it. My family met Ravi, but my parents seemed quite disinterested in my relationship with him. I avoided spending anything other than very minimal time with them because I felt ashamed about Ravi seeing my mother when she was drunk. There was no issue for any of my friends or family about the fact that Ravi was a person of colour and from a different culture. Some of my friends were relieved to actually meet him in person, having wondered, in jest, whether this invisible boyfriend might actually be a figment of my imagination. A few of my friends used to think that Ravi was probably secretly married and that this was why he had refused to meet them and my family, or introduce me to anyone he knew. I could see how this might be a reasonable deduction on their part, but I never did think that might be true. For all of his reluctance and fears about our relationship, I never once had a sense that he lied to me. He could at times be brutal in his honesty. I knew that I could phone his apartment on the off-chance at any time of the day or night and he would always freely answer unless he was at work.

After living in the flat for just over six months, my friend Cissie and her husband Dev asked if I and the twins would like to move in with them for a while. Cissie and Dev are very close friends – they are godparents to Evie and Daniel, and I am godmother to their daughter Maya. Their idea was that I would be helping them out financially by paying some rent, and that when I was ready to move out, I would be in a better position to apply to the local council for housing as we would be a bit overcrowded in their three-bedroom house. This seemed like a great idea to me, so I moved in, accepting that I would be sharing a double mattress on the floor of their small third bedroom with Evie and Daniel because I knew it would be a temporary situation.

Evie, Daniel and I shared a few happy months living with Cissie and Dev, especially as the twins were very close to Maya, being around the same age. At first, it all seemed a bit like being on a holiday, sharing lovely meals and having fun together. However, after a while, I noticed that Ravi seemed to be very reluctant to visit me there. He hated the relative loss of our privacy, although whenever he stayed at the house, Evie and Daniel would sleep in a spare bed in Maya's room, or he would come to me when the twins were with Rob. I did try to encourage him to spend time with us all, and sometimes he did. I would pretend to myself that we were becoming a little family, but I was feeling increasingly embarrassed because the flaws in our relationship were now much more visible to my friends, particularly Cissie and Dev. I was always trying to make excuses for Ravi.

I continued to try to encourage Ravi to think seriously about us buying a home together, but he still wasn't ready, so I decided to try to find a new place just for me and the twins. I applied to the council for housing, and was eventually offered a reasonable little three-bedroom house in a terrible area that was well known for being a hotbed of antisocial behaviour. Although it would have made good financial sense to opt for council housing because the rent would be less expensive than private rent and I would have more secure rights as a tenant, I felt that I had to provide a safer environment for my children. I didn't want them potentially being exposed to drug taking and violence, so I declined the offer from the council and I found a three-bedroom house in a better area, to rent privately and more expensively. I wanted to give Evie and Daniel a feeling of security, a proper home.

Now in my own house, Ravi and I enjoyed doing things together to make it more attractive and comfortable. He made an absolutely beautiful pine bookcase for me, from scratch, and I was amazed to see his exceptional talent at woodworking. I still have that bookcase, and I look at it most days with a mixture of awe and sadness. This process of normalisation, just doing everyday things like DIY together, did nothing to reduce the obsessive attraction that I felt towards Ravi. We still could not get enough of each other sexually, and I was entirely entranced by my love for him. There was one evening when I was making my bed after Ravi had left to go home, when I saw a single black hair from his body lying on the sheet. I could not brush it away or throw it in the bin – it was precious to me because it was part of his body. So, I picked up the hair and wrapped it carefully in a tissue, placing it in my bedside drawer. When I look back at this moment now, it does seem rather a strange thing to do, perhaps almost witchy. I share it with you now as it encapsulates and illustrates the mad, bordering on worshipful way in which I adored Ravi.

Although I knew for sure that I wanted to be with Ravi for the rest of my life, I had a nagging worry in the back of my mind that if he was to stay with me, he might not ever be able to have children of his own as, having been through infertility and IVF, I might not be able to conceive. Whenever I spoke to Ravi about this, he always reassured me that, although he would like to have children one day, it was not a deal breaker for him. I was thirty-four years old when I met him, and the clock was ticking. From time to time, I would start to push him again to make a decision about us, to make a commitment to me. The conversations remained repetitive and difficult. Each time I asked him what he was waiting for, and how would he know when he reached the point of knowing what he wanted to do, he would stall me with excuses, saying he wasn't able to think about it yet, as he had other things to think about. I asked him to tell his parents about me. He was extremely reluctant to do this, but eventually after several years he did tell his parents, probably pushed into it by having to explain to them why he was refusing much pressure to allow them to arrange a marriage for him. They were predictably very disappointed to hear that he was in a serious relationship with a divorced English mother of two, and apparently the fact that I was 'only' a nurse rather than a doctor made it even worse. In India, nurses are not very highly regarded. His father believed that I was just trying to trap Ravi into supporting another man's children. I think that my only redeeming feature was that I was a Roman Catholic, as Ravi's parents were devout Catholics. I used to ask Ravi to take me to India so that I could meet his parents. I believed that I wasn't a bad person and that, if they met me in person, they might like me, and if they could see for themselves how much I truly loved their son, they might be convinced to give our relationship their blessing.

I did eventually meet Ravi's mother when she came to the UK to visit him. Ravi didn't want me to take Evie and Daniel when I went to meet her, but I insisted that they should not be hidden. I got on well with Ravi's mother, and Evie and Daniel were impeccably behaved. After meeting me, Ravi's mother told him that she liked me very much, and she said that if he loved me, then he should marry me – she told him that she just wanted him to be happy. However, even after she had given her blessing, Ravi's commitment phobia remained resolutely intact.

Ravi made many trips to India to see his family, but he never did allow me to accompany him, despite my pleading. He would describe to me how beautiful it was, creating scenes in my mind of lush mango groves, paddy fields and golden beaches. He would always bring back gifts for me, such as little wooden elephants or sandalwood oils, but on one occasion he brought back a handful of sand that he had picked up from Kovalum beach in Kerala, in a small plastic bag. I knew that he was trying to do something kind by doing this, but this gift made me feel incredibly sad. It was like a crumb being offered from his life in India. I still have that little bag of sand in my box of mementoes.

After about a year of paying a high level of private rent each month, still having to pay for some child care, and still only receiving quite a small amount of child support money from Rob, my finances were becoming more difficult to manage. I remained determined to work part-time so that I would continue to be available to pick Evie and Daniel up from school, but I didn't have quite enough income to cover all of my expenses. I had started to rely on using a credit card to pay for essentials such as school uniforms, or even to buy food or pay some utility bills. After a few months of this, I took out a small bank loan to pay off the credit card. Then I found that, because I was having to pay back the loan

I still didn't have enough income to cover expenses, and so I would have to resort to using the credit card again. I did try to earn a small additional income by working as a freelance lecturer at a local university – I earned a grand total of £300 – but I was then penalised for this by the Inland Revenue who reduced my working tax credit payments. As the spiral into debt evolved, I felt ashamed and too embarrassed to look for help. I hid it from Ravi for a long time, then eventually told him that I would need to find some way of increasing my earnings, so I was planning to look for a full-time job and just accept that I would have to pay more for childcare. Ravi very kindly offered to give me enough money to pay off my credit card and a small bank loan. I was so grateful to him for helping me but I felt very uncomfortable at the same time as I didn't feel it was his responsibility to support me or my children financially.

Having until now kept quiet about the rather low amount of child support payment I received from Rob, because we were still playing the roles of him being the 'innocent party' and me being 'the guilty one' who deserved to be penalised, I started to explore a little about what the average amount of child maintenance payments should be. It seemed that Rob was paying significantly less than the recommended percentage of his income. I summoned up the courage to ask him to increase his financial contribution to the upbringing of his children and said that, if he didn't agree to it, I would consider contacting the Child Support Agency about his also back-paying any deficit for the time since we had split up. I was fearful of his anger, but beginning to wake up a little to realising that, even if Rob felt that I should be penalised, he had a duty to ensure that his children were not. Rob agreed to increase the amount of maintenance he paid and it did take the financial pressure off me for a while at least. I feel quite proud of myself for never having defaulted on any payments owed during all those years of living on a shoestring, but it was a hugely stressful struggle trying to keep everything afloat for so many years.

16

Give Me Just a Little More Time
(Chairmen Of The Board 1970)

My friends were starting to become concerned about me. I had often talked to my close female friends, Cissie and Annabelle, and to Michael, one of my closest friends from childhood, about my difficulties with Ravi's refusal to make a commitment to me. They couldn't understand why I remained so committed to a person who didn't seem to want to create a future with me.

"Jack, why are you doing this to yourself? It's not as if you are unattractive. You could easily meet someone else who would be thrilled to make a life with you and the twins," Cissie asked one day when we were chatting over a coffee.

"I suppose maybe that's true," I said, "but I love Ravi. I don't ever want to be with anyone else. I just can't imagine ever being with another man."

My friend Michael sent me the lyrics of the Eagles' song 'Desperado', and the sadness of the song's sentiments did resonate with me, as it seemed to encapsulate the way I was damaging myself in my relationship with Ravi.

My friends recognised that the shadow of depression was beginning to resurface, although I hadn't acknowledged this myself. I was quieter, and less interested in socialising. I felt embarrassed and a little ashamed – I imagined that my friends probably thought I was being weak. I started to talk less to my friends about Ravi, as I felt that I was repeatedly justifying Ravi's reluctance to commit by telling them about all of the things he had to think about before he could make a decision about me. As I recounted these excuses, I knew how pathetic they sounded, but I didn't want to see it. I felt that in some way I must not be good enough for Ravi, or else he would already have been able to make up his mind about whether he wanted to be with me or not. I was being kept at arm's length and it felt like rejection. I was being hidden in a corner of Ravi's life – as though I was something to be ashamed of.

I began to notice that I was again struggling to feel my usual deep empathy with the patients I saw at work. My heart was closing off to other people. I felt disengaged when patients were telling me about their emotions – I really didn't want to listen to other people's problems. This made me feel that perhaps I wasn't a very nice person, that maybe I was hard-hearted and unsympathetic. I didn't like myself much. In addition, there had been no provision made by my employers for me to have any form of counselling support or clinical supervision. I was heading down the road to burnout. I didn't recognise this at the time, so I did what I usually do when I'm unhappy, and I found a new job. On a whim I applied for a job as a medical sales representative for a pharmaceutical company. I thought that this would be a way of using my medical knowledge whilst not having to look after patients. Within three weeks of my application, I had a successful interview and was offered the job.

Again, the distraction and initial excitement of my new job gave me something else to focus on for a while. My role was to try to see GPs, so that I could inform and educate them about whichever drugs my company were promoting. Initially, I thought it was fascinating to be part of corporate culture when I had worked for so long in the National Health Service. There were many perks, such as a beautiful company car, huge conferences in 5-star hotels, lots of interesting people to meet and new things to learn. I was able to earn the same salary working part-time that I would have to work full time for in the NHS. It all seemed quite glamourous at first. However, I soon realised that most of my days at work were spent being constantly rejected by GP receptionists, as they were trying to protect their GPs. It seemed to me that reps were viewed as something of a nuisance, and were only of any use if they were financially sponsoring educational events for doctors. It was incredibly frustrating, and for a person like me who thrives on pleasing others, who needs to feel needed and helpful, it was incredibly down-heartening having to face constant rejection. Ironically, I would have earned some kudos as far as Ravi's parents were concerned, as medical representatives are much more highly respected in India than nurses!

However, as much as I felt like a square peg in a round hole when I was a pharmaceutical representative, I actually stayed in that job for almost three years, purely because I had a part-time term-time contract which allowed me to be with Evie and Daniel during all of the school holidays and not have to worry so much about childcare. Prior to this I had managed for years by juggling various childcare solutions, including childminders, after school or holiday clubs, asking my sister and my sister-in-law to help, or my friend Cissie, and Rob's parents. At one point I was paying exactly half of my part-time salary in childcare fees. Rob would only have the children on the alternate Friday nights and for one week in the year when he took them on holiday. I knew that this was part of his need to punish me for being the one who had wanted to divorce. As a very last resort I would have to ask my parents for help, but my fears about the safety of my children did turn out to be well founded because on a couple of occasions my mother's drunkenness resulted in the twins missing school and being very upset by witnessing arguments between my parents.

I used to find it interesting to observe how my parents interacted with my children. I think I was looking for clues about my own childhood. I seemed to have very few memories of being a child. There was one incident when Daniel was about two years old and had hit his head on the corner of a coffee table at my parents' house. Daniel's immediate reaction to bumping his head was to cry very loudly – a totally natural reaction of a child to a sudden injury or pain. As I picked Daniel up to soothe him, my dad started stroking the coffee table and saying "No need for all that crying now Daniel! What about the poor coffee table?" as though the coffee table might be suffering. Daniel suddenly stopped crying and he looked at my dad, and then at me with a look of confusion on his face as he tried to work out what he was supposed to do. Should he carry on crying because he was upset and hurt having hit his head, or should he now be trying to make the coffee table feel better? I knew that my dad was not being deliberately unkind – I realised that he was just trying to help Daniel to feel better by stopping him from crying, using distraction to take Daniel's focus away from his distress – but that moment gave me another insight into how I would probably have been taught to put other people's needs before my own – and to not allow myself to feel or express my own genuine reactions to life events.

By now I had been in a relationship with Ravi for almost five years. We were still completely addicted to each other sexually, but both of us were struggling with the constant theme of me waiting for him to make a decision about our future, and him feeling pressurised by me. I felt that I was always trying to almost coach him, and then I would try to lift his mood when I'd made him angry by my repetitive questioning. I suggested that perhaps he could try reading motivational self-help books, such as 'Feel the Fear and Do It Anyway' by Susan Jeffers, which I thought might help him to overcome whatever fears he had about commitment. There is a reference in the book to the story of a hungry donkey who is sitting between two bales of hay, looking from one to the other and trying to decide which one to eat. Unable to choose between the two bales because he thinks that if he chooses one, he will miss out on the other, he is meanwhile actually starving. I tried to convince Ravi that, if he actually made a choice one way or the other about how he would like his future to look, even though there would be no such thing as a perfect life, at least he would be moving forward and he would have the potential to be happy and to have a fuller life instead of this perpetual waiting. When he was quiet and seemingly unhappy, I used to try to lift his mood by putting upbeat music on, such as 'Bright Side of the Road' by Van Morrison, and try to get him to do a happy dance around the room with me. It would work for a while and make both of us laugh. As I write about this now, I can see in retrospect, and with a sad acknowledgement, that I don't recall ever seeing Ravi express real joy. We seemed to be stuck in an impasse, and from time to time when I hit a brick wall yet again with Ravi, I would tell him that I'd had enough and I would end the relationship. Each time I told myself that this was the last time. I was so tired of going round and round in a never-ending circle. Life as a single parent was in some ways hard enough without having to deal with the constant stress of a difficult relationship. I wanted to put more effort into giving my children happy childhood memories, instead of always being on some level distracted and low in mood due to worrying and fretting about Ravi.

Eventually, I was given the opportunity to buy the house I was renting, so I somehow managed to get a mortgage despite my part time salary, and I decided to commit to a future without Ravi. Evie and Daniel seemed to be happy and settled in our home, just the three of us. I decided to return to nursing, and found a new job for myself as a Practice Nurse in a local GP practice. The break from nursing had been good for me, and I now had both the renewed desire and capacity to undertake a caring role again.

After what I thought would certainly be my final separation from Ravi, I managed to avoid the temptation to contact him. I had asked him not to contact me again, and he respected my wishes. I didn't want to resurrect our relationship, and although I missed him terribly, I began to feel calmer and happier. I remained completely disinterested in trying to create a new relationship with anyone else – I simply just could not imagine it. Sometimes, men expressed an interest in me, some of whom were attractive, intelligent and kind, but I just didn't seem to be able to feel a shred of physical desire for any of them. I really didn't want another relationship – I was happier just focusing on creating a nice life for Evie, Daniel and myself. I didn't socialise much, partly as I wasn't interested in meeting people, and also because I had very little disposable income. Most evenings I stayed at home by myself, watching TV or reading. Sometimes I sat there, late at night when the twins were in bed, torturing myself with jealous thoughts about Ravi being with someone else, but I realised that I would have to learn to live with that fear and try to completely let go of my attachment to him.

17

Where Is the Love
(Roberta Flack/Donny Hathaway 1972)

Ravi and I had been apart for only a few weeks when, out of the blue one evening, I received a phone call from him. When I picked up the phone and heard his voice, I can remember having an enormous feeling of relief. Ravi apologised for phoning me when he had promised not to, but he wanted to let me know that his father had died, and that he was leaving for India the next day so that he could attend his father's funeral. I could hear the weary sadness in his voice and I felt a wave of compassion for him in his grief. I knew how much he had struggled with feelings of immense guilt about being here in England when his father was so far away in India dealing with terminal illness due to cancer – and now he would be left with regrets. I immediately offered to take Ravi to Heathrow Airport for his flight the next day. I was so desperate to see him, and as soon as he opened the door to me, we embraced gently and quietly, and I wrapped him in love as he expressed his grief. I said nothing about any of our historical relationship issues. I just wanted to be there for him and I was thrilled that we now had another excuse to get back together.

When Ravi returned from India, I picked him up from the airport and we went back to his flat. I knew that we would make love. We always did. Sex was the glue which held us together. We got straight into bed, and I revelled in the feel of his skin and the taste of his mouth. I loved the familiar smell of him. I was ecstatic in my relief at our reunion and my desire for Ravi. Previously I had always been on the contraceptive pill, but, as we had separated, I had stopped taking it. So, I had brought condoms in preparation. As the lovemaking progressed, I put my hand on his chest to create a pause.

"Wait…I'm not on the pill. You need to use a condom – I've got some," I said as I reached over for the packet of condoms I'd left on his bedside table.

"It's okay," he said, but he made no move to take the condom from me. He carried on making love.

"Hold on," I said, again gently pushing him away. "What do mean, it's okay? What if I get pregnant?" I asked.

"Then we'll get married and have a baby," said Ravi.

I was shocked. I had never known Ravi to be willing to take any kind of contraceptive risk. The thought of a pregnancy would to him have been complete disaster. We continued to make love, without a condom, and I felt a surge of such happiness at this turn of events that I couldn't quite believe it. I held him and took him inside me, with every cell in my body welcoming him.

I knew better than to try to talk with Ravi in the post coital glow, I knew not to ruin things by talking about my feelings. But to myself I had what I thought was a realisation that after all these years of procrastination, saying "I'm not sure yet," maybe Ravi's father's death had impacted on him in a profound way. Maybe it had made him think about the fragility and unpredictability of life – made him aware that time passes, and if you wait too long to act, then your time and opportunity may be gone before you know it? Maybe he had been afraid to disappoint his father by committing to a future with me and refusing to return to India? And now that his father had died, had it freed Ravi from this fear? Whatever the reason might have been behind Ravi's contraceptive risk-taking, I decided to accept it happily.

There followed for me the happiest six months of our relationship. We were back together. Something seemed to have softened in Ravi. He was grieving for his father and worried about his mother in India. But he seemed to be feeling closer to me. And I was feeling closer to him. We continued to have unprotected sex, both knowing that I was not taking the pill. Sometimes, Ravi would express some disappointment when each period started, and he began to come to visit me mid-week if I was at the most potentially fertile times in my cycle. I thought that we were trying to conceive.

Although Ravi hadn't actually made any further comments about our future together, the fact that we were risking a pregnancy was enough for me to think that his fear about a future with me had lessened and he was now ready. We never discussed how he felt about the prospect of being a father. I felt happy and relaxed with him. He was prepared to have a baby with me. I didn't need to keep asking him about when he was going to make a decision or a commitment to me, as by his actions he had now made this commitment. There were no long pleading letters from me. Maybe in retrospect, this is why Ravi seemed softer towards me at this time – because I wasn't bugging him about my emotions. In hindsight I realise that I was foolish to base my beliefs about all this on some rather vague elements of Ravi's behaviour, but at the time I felt the most settled and secure in our relationship that I had ever been – I didn't want to risk losing this new feeling of some semblance of peace and contentment.

I started taking folic acid and eating more healthily in readiness for a possible conception. I refused to drink alcohol. After having IVF to conceive my twins, although the reason for my failure to conceive had been unexplained and I was now thirty-nine years old, I wondered if there may still be a slight chance that I might get pregnant. I was having regular periods. I could feel little twinges of pain during ovulation and could see the changes in my cervical mucus during the middle of my cycle. I felt fertile. I was having wonderful fulfilling sex with a man I adored. I loved my body. I felt sexy and womanly. Ravi adored my body and he thrilled in my capacity for sexual response.

After six months, my period was late. I didn't feel any different, other than the absence of the usual uncomfortable dragging sensation in my pelvis just prior to menstruation. I told Ravi that my period hadn't come, one evening whilst we were chatting on the phone mid-week. Ravi didn't say anything in response to this. Almost jokingly, I told him that if my period hadn't started by the weekend when he was due to come to see me, I thought that I should do a pregnancy test. I didn't seriously believe that I was pregnant, but it felt exciting to fantasise about the possibility of it.

On the Friday evening, Ravi arrived at my house. Evie and Daniel were with Rob that weekend. I wasted no time before telling Ravi that my period still hadn't started. He was very quiet. I gave him a big hug, like I was trying to reassure or comfort him, and I asked him to come upstairs with me. I wanted to do the pregnancy test straight away – couldn't wait a minute longer. If there was even a slight chance that the test might be positive, I wanted us to discover it together.

"No...I'll wait downstairs," Ravi said. I felt a slight disappointment at this, but I knew intuitively that it would not help if I tried to pressurise him. I accepted his decision and went upstairs by myself. I should have taken this as an ominous sign.

I took the pipette from the test kit and withdrew a few drops of my urine from a pot. My hands were shaking. I paused for a second, steeling myself for what I felt was likely to be a sense, familiar from the past, of crushing disappointment. I still didn't have any symptoms of pregnancy, other than the missed period. My body didn't feel different. I dripped the urine onto the test strip and took a deep breath, feeling my heart battering against my ribs as I did so. I placed the palm of my hand on my chest, trying to calm the palpitations of my heart.

I watched the pink colour slowly spread along the white of the test strip. One bright pink line appeared, and then to my utter amazement, a second line formed. Bold and clear. I gasped and stared at it, unable to believe what I was seeing. I sat for a few seconds, perched on the side of the bath as still as a statue, my breaths rapid and shallow. The test was positive. I was pregnant.

"Oh my God, Oh my God, Oh my God..." I said quietly to myself, a whispered mantra expressing sheer joy and amazement. It felt to me that a miracle had occurred, that all of my prayers had been answered. I thought that this was a gift from God. In a single moment, the anxious fear which I had carried for all the years we had been together, that if

Ravi stayed with me, he would never have children of his own, just disappeared. I did not need to worry any more. I was actually pregnant! I felt so proud of myself and my body.

I jumped up from the side of the bath and picked up the test strip. Bounding down the stairs I couldn't wait for one more second to tell Ravi. I found him standing in front of the kitchen window, staring at the garden. He turned towards me and I threw myself towards him like an excited puppy, wrapping my arms around his neck and crying with relief and joy.

"Look!" I said as I handed the pregnancy test strip to him. "I'm pregnant! There are two stripes!"

Ravi looked at the test strip and then looked at me. He was silent. His face was unsmiling. I fell from my elated cloud with a sudden thud which shocked me to the core. Even before he spoke, the rush of fear coursing through my veins made me feel as though my whole body was in shock.

"What's wrong?" I asked.

After a moment, Ravi replied. "This is terrible…I…we… can't have a baby now."

"What do you mean, we can't have a baby now? I'm pregnant! This is a miracle…it's a gift from God that we could hardly have dared to believe possible!" I replied, my voice shaking with panic.

"I'm not ready…we are not even married," Ravi said, looking down at the floor.

My heart was pounding with a sickening fear. I couldn't connect what was happening with any sense of reality. Ravi's reaction just did not make any sense to me. In my panic, I decided to simply ignore his negativity – to try to create a shift in Ravi's response by being positive. I grabbed both of his hands in mine.

"Ravi – look at me." I said as I did a little jump like an excited child.

"Come on, don't be scared! It's amazing! I'm pregnant! It's the most fantastic thing that could have happened – it really is a miracle. I want you to be happy! You're going to be a father!" I exclaimed, trying to get Ravi to jump with me too and be excited. Ravi dropped my hands and stood resolutely still. I slumped down onto the sofa, stunned by his reaction. I said nothing, holding my breath.

Ravi sat down next to me. He took my hand gently and looked at me.

"Jackie…how about if we terminate this pregnancy, then we can get married and try for another pregnancy straight after that?"

I gasped in response.

"What?! I can't believe you just said that! Are you being serious? I am forty years old. I had IVF to conceive Evie and Daniel. I have never fallen pregnant naturally until now. This is a miracle – and it might never happen again," I said as I took my hand away from his.

I stood up and looked down at him.

"I thought you wanted me to get pregnant?" I asked as reality began to dawn on me.

"I didn't really think that it would happen, you were infertile before," Ravi said.

"So, for the past six months you have been just playing along with me like some kind of sick game?" I asked.

"No, it's not like that, I just didn't think it would happen. I'm not ready."

I stormed out of the room, started crying with gulping sobs, and went upstairs to lie on my bed with my face to the wall. Ravi followed me after a minute or so.

"I'm sorry," he said.

"Just FUCK OFF!" I hissed through gritted teeth, keeping my back turned to him. "Leave me alone."

He walked out of the room and then I heard him leave the house.

I placed my two hands on my lower abdomen and said, both to myself and to the baby inside me, "Don't worry... everything will be okay. He's just a bit shocked...he just needs a bit of time...he will come round."

Already I was a mother protecting and reassuring my unborn child, and trying to reassure myself at the same time.

I remember that, as I lay there, I repeatedly had a fleeting mental image of a little girl presenting a very special gift which she had made especially for her parents and being told that the gift was just rubbish, watching the parents sling the gift heartlessly into a bin, or being ignored despite having made such a huge effort. I didn't realise it at the time, but years later I learned through psychotherapy that this tiny fragment of an image was a message from my subconscious, which was demonstrating something very important about the dynamics of my relationship with Ravi.

18

Thin Line Between Love and Hate

(The Persuaders 1971)

I spent the next few days in a state of absolute confusion. I could not comprehend Ravi's reaction to the pregnancy. I tried to talk to him about it – to explore his fears and reassure him. I was pleading with him and trying to cajole him into changing his mindset. I wanted Ravi to be happy about the fact that we were going to have a baby together. However, he was resolute in his wish for me to have an abortion. He told me that he was not willing to support me if I went ahead with the pregnancy – he said he didn't want to be a distant father. I didn't tell anyone about what was happening. Not even my closest friends. I didn't want anyone to think badly of Ravi. I believed that he would come round to the idea and accept my pregnancy, so then there would be no need for anyone to know about his initial reaction. Soon, I was starting to notice my body changing. My breasts felt full. I could feel heat and fullness deep in my pelvis. I had waves of nausea.

I was feeling huge cascades of joy flooding my heart when I thought about the new life that was growing inside my body.

Conceiving Ravi's baby was so different to conceiving through IVF. The sperm had come directly from his body into mine – swimming up through my cervix and into my uterus. Probably the fertilisation had occurred in the warmth and safety of one of my fallopian tubes, and then the little fertilised embryo had travelled down and nestled into the nurturing home of my uterus. It was just as nature intended, in stark contrast to the experience of IVF. I knew exactly whose baby I was carrying – mine and Ravi's baby, conceived by some kind of miracle inside my own body, through passionate lovemaking.

I carried on going to work, looking after Evie and Daniel, surviving the days and trying to keep the waves of terror at bay. At night I would lay in bed with my hands placed protectively over my lower abdomen, smiling as I imagined my beautiful little Indian child beginning to form. I loved it fiercely and protectively, whilst at the same time I felt so much fear about the future that sometimes I couldn't breathe.

About a week after the positive pregnancy test, I met with Ravi again and tried to talk to him. He remained horrified about my being pregnant. I decided to make an appointment for both of us to go to a BPAS clinic in London to have some counselling about what was happening. My hope was that the counsellor might be able to help Ravi see things more positively where I had failed to do so. Unfortunately, the counselling session did nothing to shift Ravi's attitude. The counsellor just seemed to acknowledge that Ravi had an insurmountable fear about taking responsibility in this situation, and she suggested that as time was an issue regarding making a decision about termination of the pregnancy, we could book a provisional date for the procedure, in case we did decide to end the pregnancy. I agreed to this, although I still believed that it would not happen. We left the clinic with an appointment for an abortion two weeks hence.

I was in a predicament. I was pregnant with a very precious baby, a baby who was absolutely loved and wanted by me. I was a single parent of eleven-year-old twins. I was still struggling to make ends meet financially – just about managing to keep a roof over our heads and put food on the table. I was in a new job as a Practice Nurse in a GP practice. I tried to work out how I would manage with another baby entirely on my own. I checked my Practice Nurse contract and realised that I would not be entitled to any maternity pay as I hadn't been in post for long enough. I went to the Citizen's Advice Bureau to find out what I might be entitled to in the way of benefits. I was advised that, as I was working part time and technically a home owner, albeit with a mortgage, I wouldn't really be entitled to any financial assistance. I was told that if I left my job I wouldn't be entitled to benefits because I had chosen to leave voluntarily. I was afraid that, if

I had the baby, then Evie, Daniel and I might lose our home. Having moved on from putting my children through the trauma of divorce and the upheaval of living in temporary accommodation, I could see that they were finally beginning to feel settled in our home and they seemed to have adjusted to having divorced parents. They appeared to be happy, and I did not want to uproot them and make them suffer any more. I still kept thinking that Ravi would come round and he would be with me and it would all be okay.

For two weeks Ravi and I went round and round in circular conversations, trying to work out what to do.

"What if it's got Downs? You could have a disabled baby because you're older. I don't want a disabled child," Ravi said

"Yes, that's true, but it might not be disabled. Lots of women have babies in their forties and they are fine," I replied. "I could have all the tests to find out." I did feel, however, that, if Ravi and I were together, even if the baby was disabled, we would manage that, and we would still love it because it was ours.

"Would you support me financially with the baby if I go ahead with the pregnancy, even if we are not together?" I asked.

"I don't want to be an absent father," Ravi replied.

I was hitting my head against a brick wall.

The planned abortion date was looming. I felt like I was

in some kind of nightmare. Ravi came to see me a couple of times. I had stopped trying to convince him to feel happy, thinking that, if I didn't pester him, he might come round of his own accord. We stopped talking, but we still made love. It was like a compulsion for us to have sex. No matter how unhappy we were, sex always took some of the unhappiness away, gave us some temporary comfort.

"Does it feel any different?" I asked.

"Yes, it feels hotter inside," Ravi replied.

I loved this. My amazing body was growing his baby and he could sense the warmth of this creative process with his own body as he penetrated me. I didn't express this to him, but I hoped that he was sensing something too and beginning to understand how amazing it was.

It was the day before the planned date for the abortion. We had agreed that he would come to my house the night before and he would drive us to the clinic. I still didn't believe that we would actually go through with it. Evie and Daniel were with Rob for the night and wouldn't be returning until the next evening.

That night, Ravi and I lay side by side in the dark. Neither of us could sleep. We did not speak. I held my tummy and thought of my baby. I could feel my heart racing with fear. I imagined my baby's heart beating fast – in synchrony with my own heart. I pictured the two hearts that were pumping within my own body. Silent tears streamed down my face and

I felt a rising tide of nausea, making me think that I might be sick. I tried to control my breathing, but I think that Ravi knew I was crying. I thought that he might reach over and hold my hand, but he didn't. We continued to just lie there, side by side, like two statues, and for the first time since we'd been together, we shared a bed but we didn't make love.

The morning came, and Ravi and I got dressed in silence. As we left the house to go to the clinic, I slammed the front door hard behind me, showing my anger through my actions rather than words.

Ravi and I were just a few minutes into our journey, Ravi was driving. As we headed towards our appalling destination, I could sense my whole body trying to pull backwards, as though by doing this I might somehow be able to reverse the forward movement of the car. I felt weak and powerless. I gradually became aware of a strange unpleasant smell filling the car, like dirty sweat. I thought at first that the smell must be entering the car from outside through the air vents, but as the miles disappeared behind us, I realised that the smell which continued to intensify in a choking miasma was actually coming from Ravi. The smell was so thick I could almost taste it.

I could not connect the unrecognisable odour emanating from the man sitting beside me with the familiar smell of the Ravi I knew – my Ravi, who had always smelled to me like the soft clean smell of sex and love, of warm skin and bliss.

I had always adored the delicious unique scent of him, and would list amongst my greatest sensual pleasures, the joy and comfort of inhaling the scent of his body. I used to breathe him in like some kind of aphrodisiac ether. It was one of the things which I had always loved about him, the cleanliness of his body, and the reliable freshness of his beautiful skin. In that moment, I could hardly bear to breathe the air in his presence.

I lifted my wrist to my nose, trying to mask the unpleasant smell by inhaling the faint traces of perfume on my watch strap. I sat motionless in that position, until eventually I opened the car window and presented my face to the rush of the cool airstream. The flooding of saliva which had heralded nausea began to subside.

I looked at Ravi, as if to check whether it was in fact Ravi sitting next to me, although I knew it was. I felt repulsed by him, and my rage showed in a fiercely hot stare of contempt. Ravi refused to meet my eyes, and kept a fish-eyed gaze on the motorway ahead.

I hate you, I thought as I looked away from him, the rigidity of my body saying what my lips did not. This unfamiliar feeling of hostility towards him was utterly shocking to me – it seemed to be rooted somewhere very deep in my soul. Not a fleeting emotion, but firmly embedded in a place I did not recognise.

I tried to suppress the jagged rips of anger which were

rising within me. Making my heart pound and pressing a heavy ache into my chest. Until that day, throughout all the intense years of ebb and flow in our relationship, a constant thread of love had always been there to pick up on, which would always steer us both back safely to equilibrium. But I could not locate the thread of the consuming passion which had been ours for so many years. The thread was broken.

I turned slowly and looked at Ravi again. I willed him to look at me. I imagined that in a few moments he would turn to me and tell me that he was sorry. He would beg for forgiveness and acknowledge that what we intended to do was wrong. That we could not go through with the decision. He would turn off the motorway at the next junction and we would sit somewhere quietly, hugging each other and crying tears of relief. He would smile, and all would be well.

The miles continued to tick away and Ravi continued to stare at the road. He said nothing. Not a flicker of a glance in my direction. Not a trace of emotion leaked from his impassive face.

I fought the urge to speak, to scream at him in a last-minute attempt to make him aware of what we were soon to lose. I knew that it would be futile – there was nothing more to say. He had made his decision. Ravi did not want our child and never would. That we loved each other was irrelevant. That I already loved and felt the presence of the new life inside me, and that I ached with the prospect of its loss, was immaterial. The crippling fear at the very heart of Ravi, the fear of living wholeheartedly that had always imprisoned him, was insurmountable, as it always had been and probably always would be. I knew that there was no point now in begging him to change his mind.

I suddenly wondered if possibly the reason why Ravi smelled different was because he hadn't showered that morning as a result of some warped idea of self-punishment, as though because of what he was about to do he did not deserve to be clean. It was the type of thing that he would do. I realised then that what I could smell was the odour of fear, and that Ravi was probably as terrified as I was. And even in my anger, I felt a flash of compassion for this weak man, whose timid nature had always stood as an insurmountable barrier to his ability to embrace the messy and wonderful entirety of life. I lowered my head in resignation, and cried silent tears as I took the first staggering steps into mourning.

When I look back at those moments, I find it hard to understand why I allowed myself to be so powerless, like a lamb being taken to slaughter. It was as though I really did have no choice.

We were coming up to the motorway junction for the turn off to the clinic, when Ravi drove into the lane which would take us into a right turn towards the town where he lived.

"You're going the wrong way," I said.

After a pause, Ravi replied "No...I'm going the right

way."

I realised then that the moment I had been longing for had just actually happened. He had changed his mind about going to the clinic for the termination of the pregnancy. He was taking me to his apartment instead.

All of the tension I had been holding in my body began to dissipate with the huge flood of relief which washed through me. I was going to have this baby. And all would be well. "Thank God, thank God, Thank God," I said to myself, a prayer of immense gratitude.

When we got to Ravi's apartment, I phoned the clinic to tell them that we wouldn't be attending after all, so our appointment was cancelled. Ravi had gone into his bedroom, so I followed him there. When I walked into the bedroom, Ravi was sitting on the side of his bed, rocking backwards and forwards and slumped over with his head in his hands.

"Ravi, what's wrong?" I asked, thinking that maybe he was unwell.

Ravi slumped forwards even more, saying, "Oh God... what have I done?... What have I done?"

I started to feel a rising panic, the inside of my ears going cold and a vice gripping my abdomen.

"Ravi, what are you talking about?"

"I can't do this." Ravi replied. "I'm not ready."

"Move up," I said, as I tried to get him to lie on the bed so that I could lie down with him.

"Listen Ravi…there's nothing to fear," I said as I took his hand and placed it on my tummy.

"Hey, just imagine…when my tummy is huge and you place your hands on it you will feel your baby kicking in there. It will be so amazing!" I said.

Ravi passively allowed his hand to rest on me, but stared at the ceiling.

"Listen, I know that being a parent is a huge commitment, and sometimes it's hard work, but it really is unbelievably wonderful too. Trust me. You have no idea how incredible it will be when you see your own baby being born. There is so much joy to come," I said.

I wanted Ravi to be like one of those men you see on TV and in films, who tenderly caress their partner's pregnant bump, feeling excitedly for the baby's movements, and lovingly talking to their unborn child. I wanted Ravi to treat me as somebody precious who was carrying his beautiful child, for him to understand the gift that my body was creating inside me. But Ravi just wasn't capable of being that man. I wanted him to say something, to laugh at how ridiculous he was being, but he remained silent. I sat up on the bed and looked at him.

"Look, Ravi, if what's worrying you is the fact that you think we can't have a baby if we are not married, because of what your family would think, it's really not a problem. We can get married if you like! Look, instead of freaking out here, why don't we stop all this panicking and do something positive? We could go into town now and buy two wedding rings!" I said, laughing and trying to lighten the mood as I stood up from the bed.

Ravi sat up on the side of the bed again, and I could see that he looked even more stricken with fear after listening to my efforts to reassure him. His face looked ashen – almost grey. And as I watched him, that was the moment when I made the worst decision I have ever made in my entire life. I looked at Ravi sitting hunched over and in despair, and I felt utter contempt towards him.

"You...are a pathetic...FUCKING...moron. You...really are...a waste of space as a man...I HATE you," I thought as the cold shadow of reality draped itself over me.

As I looked at him, a thought went through my mind that, if I had this baby, I would be connected to him for the rest of my life. In that moment, I felt such hatred towards him that I truly wanted never to have anything to do with him again. In that precise moment of what seemed like complete clarity, I made the decision to terminate the pregnancy.

I walked out of the bedroom without saying anything to Ravi. I left him sitting there on his bed. He didn't try to stop me. I waited for a while in the other room, stunned with grief, not knowing what to do. As I didn't have my car there, I considered trying to get home by taking a train into London and then another one to my home, but I was so wiped out with sadness that I didn't have the physical energy to make the journey. So, when Ravi eventually came into the room, I asked him to drive me home. I don't remember anything about that journey – I must have been in a state of numb shock. When we arrived outside my house, Ravi parked the car and I got out without speaking. I didn't even have the strength to slam the car door behind me. Ravi turned the car around and drove off. Later that evening, Rob dropped the children back, and I don't know how I managed to get through the rest of the evening.

Evie and Daniel could sense that something was awry. "What's wrong, mum?" they asked several times.

"Nothing. I'm fine," I lied in response each time.

The next day I phoned the clinic in London and re-booked a date for the termination. I survived on auto-pilot for those few days. Ravi phoned me to ask if I was okay. We didn't chat for long. I had nothing more to say to him, other than to tell him that I had re-booked an appointment for the abortion. Ravi offered to take me to the clinic and to pay for the abortion. I wanted to never have to see him again, but I decided to allow him to accompany me so that he could be a witness to the grief that he had caused me.

19

Love Don't Live Here Anymore
(Faith Evans 1995)

On September 17th in the year 2000, in a clinic far from my home, I signed a consent form and allowed an anaesthetist to administer a general anaesthetic so that a doctor could use a suction machine to remove my nine-week fetus from my womb. I can remember a sense of having to force myself into some sort of trance, to disconnect from myself, in order to allow it to happen. Ravi drove me home after the abortion. We were silent, both of us completely shocked and speechless after what had just happened. I had asked my friend, Cissie, to look after Evie and Daniel for me whilst I was at the clinic. I had told Cissie where I was going. She and her husband were the only people who knew at this time. When I got to their house, Cissie answered the door and looked at me with such compassion that the wall around me that contained my grief began to crumble. Cissie didn't speak – she just put her arms around me and held me, like a mother would. My own eyes were dry and my heart was like stone. I was paralysed with grief. I took Evie and Daniel home, fielding their questions as they tried to work out why I was so quiet.

"I'm just upset about my mum," I said. They knew that I was often upset about my mother and the impact of her alcoholism, so they accepted my excuse.

That awful day formed for me a threshold between the existence of hope and the first steps of an unbearable journey into the unrelenting and grinding despair of grief. I don't remember much detail about the day itself. The mind has a clever mechanism for self-protection, and when a person is in a state of being absolutely overwhelmed due to traumatic experiences, the brain doesn't create memories in the normal ways. I suspect that the memories of that day will thankfully have been buried somewhere in the dark and inaccessible recesses of my mind.

The following day I dropped Evie and Daniel off at school. Then I sat at home all day as I didn't work on Mondays. I was motionless – a catatonic statue. It was as though I had been frozen. I didn't eat. I didn't drink. I couldn't sleep. I could feel period type pains because my womb was contracting. I was bleeding slightly, but no more than I would have expected. Ravi didn't call me. I didn't want him to.

By the evening, my bleeding was beginning to get heavier. I got Evie and Daniel to bed and tried to relax in a warm bath as the pains were getting worse. When I got out of the bath, I passed a large blood clot the size of a plum. Then I passed another big clot. I was beginning to feel faint. At this point I started to become frightened, as I thought that I might be haemorrhaging due to the presence of some remnants of pregnancy tissue in my uterus. I didn't know what to do. I thought that I might need to go to the hospital to get help. I was afraid that the hospital staff in the Emergency Department, some of whom I knew, would judge me, as I would have to tell them that I'd had an abortion. I felt ashamed. I wondered whether to phone Cissie to see if she would come to mind the children whilst I went to the hospital. I decided to phone Ravi and tell him. He seemed worried, but he advised me to keep an eye on the bleeding and see if it settled on its own. He offered to come up to see me if I wanted him to. I resolutely didn't want to see him, so I declined his offer.

I took some ibuprofen and after an hour or so of heavy blood loss, the bleeding began to reduce and the pain subsided. I went to bed and prayed that I wouldn't bleed any more. I was too afraid to sleep.

The next day I had to go to work. I felt unwell. I looked pale with dark circles under my eyes and I felt dizzy whenever I moved. I realised that I might be slightly anaemic after the blood loss. All I wanted to do was to get into bed, to lie still, and to be able to cry some of the pain out of my crushed and broken heart, but I had to get up and somehow get through the day. I needed to get the twins to school and myself to work. I considered whether to call in sick, but I was worried that my colleagues might think badly of me and I would be letting them down, as I had a fully booked clinic. As I was in a new job, I didn't dare to risk making a bad impression.

My first session of the day was a baby immunisation clinic. It was absolutely the last thing I needed. The first woman came in with her eight-week-old baby for his first immunisations. I administered the vaccines and tried to maintain a professional stance during the consultation. The baby was crying after the injections, so the mother asked if I would mind if she fed him for a minute to calm him down. I told her that would be fine, but as I watched her put the baby to the breast, I wanted to howl with grief. I wanted to run out of the room and shout and scream at the horror and pain of the loss of my own baby. I made a huge conscious effort to swallow my feelings and looked away from the mother and tried to concentrate on filling in the paperwork. Somehow, I managed to finish the rest of the clinic.

I still hadn't told anyone other than Cissie about the abortion. It was partly from my own feelings of shame and the need to keep my feelings locked away somewhere in order to cope with my daily responsibilities, but I still felt that I didn't want anyone to think badly of Ravi. I remained in a kind of numb state emotionally for about two weeks and managed to go to work, and to look after Evie and Daniel. One day I was at work and I went in to ask one of the female doctors, Claire, for some advice about a patient.

"Come in and sit down," she said. "One of my patients hasn't turned up."

I sat down in the chair opposite the doctor's desk.

"Are you ok?" the doctor asked.

"Yes…why?" I asked.

"I don't know, you seem a bit on edge," she said.

I was quiet for a few seconds and then I said I had to get back to my patient. I turned towards the door so that the doctor wouldn't see the glistening of tears in my eyes.

After the clinic was finished, I went in to the doctor's room again and asked if I could speak to her. I proceeded to tell her what had happened. I could not stop crying. Claire stood up and put her arm around my shoulders. She remained silent whilst I continued to cry. Then she told me that I could talk to her at any time if I felt that I needed to, and reassured me that it would be okay if I felt I needed to take some time off work. She said she wouldn't tell anyone what I'd shared with her and that I could make up some other excuse as to why I was absent from work.

I didn't take time off work. I have always been absolutely conscientious, perhaps too conscientious, about my professional commitment to work, never feeling comfortable about letting my colleagues down. This has sometimes been to my own detriment and to that of others around me. I think in retrospect that I probably should have taken a little time away from work to try to process my grief, as I found that, once I had opened the floodgates by sharing my story with my GP colleague, I started telling anyone and everyone I met, apart from my patients and my family. It was all spilling out of me. I would tell my story to professional colleagues, people I didn't even know, when I met them at medical meetings. I could sense that when I shared so inappropriately with these relative strangers about something so personal, they looked uncomfortable and tried to break the conversation. I didn't care by then what people thought about Ravi. The lights had gone out in my eyes and I didn't know how to speak to people any more. I had lost my sense of self and didn't know how to relate with others. I think I had some kind of need to explain to them why I seemed to be so disconnected and dead-eyed. I had always seen myself as a warm and open person, a good communicator who could connect with everyone I met. Now I felt like a horrible, cold person. I needed people to know that I wasn't really a bad person, but I was someone who had been damaged and hurt. Then maybe they would feel sorry for me rather than dislike me, God forbid.

Unfortunately, this period of totally inappropriate emotional incontinence lasted for several months. It didn't occur to me to get any professional psychological help at that time. I managed to continue going to work and to care for Evie and Daniel's needs, but at night when they were in bed I would sit downstairs in the silence, ruminating over a recurrent image of my baby screaming in pain as it was being ripped to pieces and torn from my uterus. I kept replaying this vision over and over again, and then I would feel that I wanted to roar from somewhere deep down inside me, like a wounded animal, but I muffled the sounds with a cushion so that I didn't wake the children. Each time the emotional pain hit an unbearable peak, I would start hitting and slapping my legs as hard as I could in order to try to reduce the awful magnitude of this pain and prevent myself from crying out loud. I had bruises and slap marks all over my thighs. I didn't consider self-harming by actually cutting my skin, but I gained an insight in those moments as to how people who self-cut might be driven to do this – it is a desperate and instinctive attempt to stop unimaginable psychological pain. Sometimes, when I lay in bed at night, I allowed thoughts about suicide to float into my consciousness. I didn't know how I was going to survive this heartbreak and still function. There seemed to be no relenting of it. I wanted the torment of grief to stop, and I thought that, if I died, then I wouldn't feel the pain of grief any more.

I had a strong sense of my lost baby being a little tiny soul, floating and lost somewhere in heaven, all alone, and, if I died, I would be reunited with it. That is if I actually did get to heaven following my death, after what I had done. I pondered how I would actually take my own life. If I was to take an overdose, when and where would I do it? Who would

I want to find me? Which of my friends would be best able to cope with it? Should I subtly try to ask someone in advance who would care for Evie and Daniel if I died? I didn't feel that I could assume that Rob would take them in. I thank God now that my love for my two existing children was strong enough to be the main reason why I didn't attempt suicide. I knew that no matter how bad my own distress was, I could not inflict the suffering of the loss of their mother on them. My mess was not their fault, and they did not deserve to suffer any more than they had already because of my failings and my lack of strength.

At this time, I used to take my children to mass at a local Catholic church. Although my own connection to Catholicism was very much a pick and mix approach because there was a lot about the teachings of the church with which I didn't agree, I had to take Evie and Daniel to mass, as they were attending a Catholic school. Each time I stood in the church, I felt that I should not be there after what I had done. I had taken the life of my own child, and in the eyes of the church this was a mortal sin at the most profound level. Strangely, although I felt so guilty, I used to feel at the same time that I was in some strange way drawn to be there when I looked at the statue of Jesus on the cross. I had a sense of his forgiveness. I have never thought of God as a vengeful punishing deity, rather I think of God as a being of pure and unconditional love. I picture Jesus as a real person, with hairs on the backs of his hands and dusty feet, and at times of confusion I sometimes imagine sitting on a park bench with him and asking him what I should do. My own version of prayer, I suppose.

One of the hardest things about being at mass was that there were always so many babies present. One day, a young couple was seated in front of me with their small baby girl, aged around three months, I guessed. The man was white, and the woman had darker skin, I thought perhaps she might have been from the Philippines. She was holding the baby over her shoulders and the baby was looking directly at me. I could not take my eyes off this child. She had honey coloured skin and glossy pure black hair. I was standing so close to her that I could pick up her soft baby scent. The baby gazed at me steadily with her huge brown eyes and I tortured myself as I imagined what my own baby would have been like. My baby never had a chance to look at the world through his or her eyes. He or she would have been of mixed race, with a combination of my pale Irish skin and Ravi's beautiful brown skin. He or she would in all likelihood have had light brown skin and dark brown eyes. I looked at the baby's perfect hands and I thought of Ravi's beautiful hands, which I had always loved. At the image I conjured up of my baby's hands, I became light-headed and thought that I might faint, so I sat down.

"Mum, are you okay?" Evie asked, concerned that I had

sat down at a point in the mass where we weren't supposed to.

"Yes, I'm okay, darling, I just feel a bit hot. Don't worry."

After mass, the priest, Father John, was standing outside saying goodbye to the congregation as they left the church. He and I had become good friends over the years.

"Hi, Jacqueline! How are you doing?" he asked as the twins and I went over to say hello to him.

Without any prior thought, and I didn't know why I decided to do it, I asked in a whisper if I could meet with him on my own for face-to-face confession. I think maybe I was feeling desperate to find some way of taking the weight of this unrelenting guilt away from my shoulders.

I met with the priest during the following week, in a quiet and private room in the presbytery. I told him all about the abortion and about the relationship with Ravi. I trusted Father John well enough to know that he would not be unkind to me but, given his position as a Roman Catholic priest and the attitude of the church towards abortion, I was astounded by the compassion and loving understanding which he showed towards me. He did not speak about punishment or guilt or shame, but focussed instead on acknowledging my enormous grief about the loss of my unborn child. He spoke about the miracle of pregnancy and the sacredness of this process in the female body, and how he could understand the enormity of my sadness that this natural process of procreation had been stopped by me when I was so utterly unsupported in my relationship with Ravi. I cried so much at being held emotionally in such a loving space by this kind and gentle man.

Gradually, the acutely painful traumatic thoughts and recurrent visualisations about the torn-up fetus began to occur less frequently. But I still found it very hard to look at a pregnant woman or a baby without feeling distressed. As a rule, society celebrates and gets all gooey-eyed about pregnancy and babies. Mothers are revered and put on a pedestal. With my negative feelings I felt again that I was at odds with the rest of society. I felt jealous and angry and couldn't conjure up any genuine expressions of joy towards others in this regard. I used to wonder what sort of horrible person I must be. When I had conceived my twins, I'd been cured of all this negativity. I had felt so happy that I was part of the club of motherhood, of women who are loved and respected just by virtue of the fact that they are mothers. At last, I had been able to love other women's babies again and to feel genuine joy when pregnancies were announced. I was a normal woman. After the abortion, all this was once more lost to me. And this made me feel so sad and ashamed of myself.

I do not remember talking to Ravi for many months after the abortion, but he has since told me that he did in fact come to visit me a few weeks after the event, as he was worried about me. He told me that I had shouted and screamed at him and told him in no uncertain terms to get away from me and never to contact me again. I had often thought in retrospect how strange it was that I never expressed anger directly towards Ravi. Sadness, disappointment, frustration yes, but the expression of real direct and heartfelt anger, I could not recall. It's very interesting to me that this event happened and that I genuinely have no recollection of it. I must have been so traumatised by the expression of my anger that I have repressed this memory. This was an important piece of learning for me about my fear of anger.

In the early aftermath of the abortion, I didn't do anything much other than merely survive. I went to work and looked after Evie and Daniel. I had no interest in socialising. I occasionally met with Cissie and Annabelle. They were both very supportive towards me, although, as a Christian, Annabelle expressed great sadness that I hadn't shared with her that I was planning an abortion before it actually happened, as she felt that she could have helped me to see how I could have continued with the pregnancy and been supported by people other than Ravi. I feel sad as I look back now and see how entrenched my self-sufficient behaviour was – how it hadn't even occurred to me to reach out to others for help when I was in such a difficult situation.

Even though I had insisted that I never wanted to see Ravi again, I missed him. Even though I was angry with him, I still remembered how much I had loved him and how I'd thought that we would be together for life. I had believed that he was my soul mate. I wondered if he was suffering too. I was longing to speak to him but I kept my resolve and didn't contact him. I missed his physical presence and I missed making love with him. In addition to grieving for the loss of my unborn baby, I was bereaved by the loss of my relationship with Ravi. I felt shut down and lonely, but despite various attempts by my friends to get me to go out and meet new people, perhaps find a new relationship, I still had no desire whatsoever to be with anyone else.

I renewed my efforts to focus my attention on Evie and Daniel by spending quality time with them and finding ways to make good memories. Although we could never afford a proper holiday, I managed to get enough money together to take them for a weekend at Alton Towers with an overnight stay in a hotel. It wasn't a particularly great experience for the three of us, as there were many rides where each child needed to be accompanied by an adult, so I couldn't go on the ride with just one of the twins and leave the other alone on the ground.

I often found that when I was out somewhere with the children, for example at a park, I would look at other families where there was a mum and a dad, and I would feel pangs of sadness about the breakdown of my marriage to Rob. I didn't go as far as feeling regret about the divorce, but just a feeling of sadness that we were not together as a family with our children. I felt sad for Rob, sad for me, and mainly sad for our children. I tried to imagine that, if Ravi and I had managed to make our relationship work in a committed and stable way, perhaps he would have been able to be a father figure for my children and help me to care for them. I have to admit that this little fantasy could never quite be fully pictured in my mind, as Ravi had always seemed to be disconnected from and disinterested in my children.

20

Try a Little Tenderness

(Otis Redding 1966)

After a few months, I began to try to open my mind to the possibility of a new relationship. I really couldn't imagine being with anyone other than Ravi, but I felt so lonely and bored with my own company. With the encouragement of my friends, I decided to try online dating. I met a few men in whose company I sat for an hour or two, whilst waiting for the most opportune moment to leave, as I wasn't at all interested in them. There was one man, Peter, who did seem like a potential prospect as a partner. Peter and I met in a pub for our first date. He was quite attractive, although not what I would have described as the type I would usually be attracted to. He was Scottish, with greying sandy-blonde hair, very softly spoken, and he seemed very genuine and kind. We met for a second date, when just as we were saying goodbye, he tried to kiss me and I froze. I couldn't do it. I felt I would be betraying Ravi, to whom I had never been unfaithful. I retreated back into myself after that. I wasn't ready.

At this time, my mother's alcoholism was becoming even more of a problem. She was at times being violent to my father and there had been a few episodes where one or the other of them had been injured, ending up in visits to the A&E. I managed to persuade my father to attend an Al Anon group with me. Al Anon is a national organisation that provides help and support to family and friends who are affected by the alcohol dependency of someone in their lives. My father and I didn't know what to do to make things better. At night my father would sleep in a separate room, as my mum would be up drinking and roaming around the house in the early hours. My mother felt rejected by my father's refusal to share a bed with her, and she would go into the room where he was sleeping and torment him, sometimes throwing water over him on the bed to express her anger. My poor father was exhausted. Someone in the Al Anon group suggested he could put a lock on the door of the spare bedroom to prevent my mother from entering the room and disturbing him. My father did reluctantly put a lock on the door, but unfortunately, my mother kicked the door in whilst in a fit of temper and she broke the lock. I was afraid that something terrible would happen, even that my mother might kill my father. There had already been one incident when she had spent a night in police custody after assaulting him. The police tried to encourage my father to press charges, but he refused to do it. I tried to encourage him to leave her and come to stay with me, but each time he would go back to her after hearing her drunken rambling messages on my answerphone, threatening that she would kill herself if he didn't return.

I asked for an on-call GP to come out to the house on two occasions, as I thought maybe, if they could admit my mother to the psychiatric hospital, they would be able to stop her drinking. On one of these occasions, we were so desperate to get help, and so afraid that someone would come to harm, because my mother was being very aggressive and agitated, that whilst we were waiting for the doctor to arrive at the house and my mother was threatening to run off, I pinned her down on the floor and held her there until the doctor arrived. We struggled terribly, but I was the stronger of the two of us, so I managed to contain her there for some time. It makes me feel ashamed to think about that episode now, but I was absolutely distraught with panic. The doctor refused to admit her to a psychiatric hospital whilst she was drunk. I spoke to a kind woman from the Police Domestic Violence Unit. She said that there was nothing the police could do if we didn't want to press charges, but they did put my father's phone number on a red alert, so that if he needed help urgently, he could just dial 999 and they would send someone to the house without him having to speak, as my mother would always snatch the phone from him whenever he tried to call for help.

One thing which the Al Anon group did teach me was how to accept my mother as she was, and how to love her with detachment. I tended to react to her angrily most of the time, wanting her to change her behaviour and to be the mother I needed her to be. Al Anon taught me that I was powerless to change my mother, and that the only thing I did have power over was my own thoughts, behaviour and reactions. I learned to understand that she had an illness, and that she was not just wilfully being horrible to everyone around her. I began to comprehend that she too was suffering, and very gradually my angry feelings towards her evolved into more of a sense of compassion. Instead of arguing with her and telling her how badly I thought she was behaving when she was drunk, I simply removed myself from the situation each time, quietly protecting myself from becoming distressed by what I was witnessing. When my mother had quieter moments, I was able to remain in her presence and I made deliberate attempts to try to be kind to her.

I had no memories of any physical contact as a little girl with my mother, apart from one time in very early childhood when she rubbed some Vicks ointment on my chest when I had a cold. I didn't feel that I could put my arms around her, it would have felt like too much for both of us, somehow false, but I wanted to find a way of connecting with her. Perhaps I hoped that I might heal her with my kindness. One day, I summoned up the courage and offered to give her a manicure. I thought that it might help her to feel that I cared for her. As we sat quietly, she allowed me to massage cream into her dry hands, and to file, shape and paint her nails, and now that precious moment has become one of my most cherished memories.

I tried to express concern about my mother's drinking, rather than condemn her with my negative judgements. My mother had never herself acknowledged that she had a problem with alcohol. She seemed to be in complete denial and blamed everyone else around her for her anger. One day, I was at my parents' house quite early in the morning, and my mother seemed very subdued. I took the opportunity of this quiet moment to tell her that I was worried that the amount of alcohol that she drank might be harming her physical health, her liver in particular. I was amazed when my mother agreed to ask her GP for a blood test to check her liver function. When the results of this blood test did actually show some abnormalities, I think it frightened her. I tentatively suggested that I could help to arrange for her to talk to someone professional who would understand about alcohol dependency and recovery. I was very surprised when she agreed to do this. It was the first time that she gave any hint of accepting that she had a problem. I managed to quickly arrange an appointment for her at a local Drug and Alcohol service. At my mother's request, I accompanied her to the appointment.

In the waiting room, my mother was pacing around and very agitated, like a caged animal. I imagine that she must have been incredibly nervous. Like my father, she was a very private person who didn't appreciate other people knowing her business. The counsellor called us in. I noticed her long flowing skirt and dangly wooden giraffe earrings, and thought to myself, rather judgementally, that she looked almost like a parody of the kind of therapist one might portray in a comedy sketch. My mother sat on the edge of her chair, almost hyperventilating. I looked at the counsellor, who placed her hands on her lap, then tilted her head to one side, as though she was deliberately adopting a position of sympathy.

"Well, Maeve," the counsellor said, softly. "What can you tell me about alcohol and all the problems that you have with it?"

My mother stood up and hissed at the counsellor, "I'm not listening to this!" She proceeded to open the door and exited the room with an angry flourish.

I was so disappointed and angry with the counsellor. I wished that she had approached the subject of alcohol more subtly, to have spent a little time just getting to know my mother, rather than hitting her straight away with what must have felt to her like an accusation. I never did manage to get my mother to seek help after that, and her dependence on alcohol continued to worsen over subsequent years.

As I was the eldest child, my father would always turn to

me first to seek help and support when things were kicking off with my mother. My younger brother and sister were comparatively uninvolved. One day, my father phoned to say that my mother had fallen and hit her head on a doorframe, and that she had left the house bleeding from a scalp wound. I drove straight round to their house, frightened about what I might find when I got there. My father was very distressed, worried about where my mum had gone. I drove around the estate where they lived, until I eventually saw my mother staggering along the pavement. She looked a pitiful sight. She was dishevelled, and her face and blouse were covered in blood. I stopped the car but she wouldn't get in. After giving up trying to persuade her, I went back to my parents' house and waited with my father in the hope that my mother would return home. She eventually turned up, and as her head wound was still bleeding, I managed to convince her that she needed to go to the hospital, as it needed stitching. I covered the passenger car seat with plastic bin liners to protect it from being stained with blood, and took my mother to the local accident and emergency unit. I felt so ashamed of her in front of the hospital staff, as the small cubicle where we waited was filled with the smell of stale alcohol from her breath – redolent of the times I had worked in the department as a student nurse, looking after drunken patients when they'd been injured in alcohol fuelled brawls.

21

Shout

(The Isley Brothers 1959)

I was finding it increasingly difficult to cope with the combination of the stressful factors in my life. There was the ongoing impact of my mother's alcoholism and trying to support my father through this. I was working so hard as a single parent, yet always struggling to manage financially. I couldn't seem to find a way to come to terms with the unremitting grief about the termination and the loss of my relationship with Ravi. There was a boiling well of rage simmering constantly underneath the surface of the veneer which I presented to the world, and I was exhausted trying to keep the lid on it. Sometimes, after I'd dropped Evie and Daniel at school, I would drive to a quiet spot with nobody around, park the car, and then scream as loudly as I possibly could, trying to get rid of the corrosive anger inside me. One day I did this so loudly that I actually lost my voice for a few hours afterwards. I'd probably caused some trauma to my vocal cords. I also used to take glass jars and bottles which I'd saved up for recycling, and I would throw them hard and furiously into the bottle bank, hurling them as hard as I could into the bins and relishing the loud noise of them smashing. These seemed like safe ways to release my anger without harming anyone around me. At my friend Annabelle's suggestion, I went for a few hypnotherapy sessions in an attempt to learn how to manage my anger more safely. The hypnotist asked me to create a visual image to represent my anger. I pictured a conical flask, like the ones we used to use in chemistry lessons in school, full of boiling purple liquid, and the flask was sitting above a high Bunsen burner flame. I imagined that the purple fluid represented my anger, and it was spitting out all over the place from the neck of the flask, damaging everything around it. The hypnotherapist asked me to visualise that there was a dial under the burner which I could adjust to turn the flame down, and to imagine that as I reduced the flame, the purple fluid stopped boiling until it was completely still. This exercise proved to be quite powerfully effective at helping my rage to subside – when I remembered to use it – and I still sometimes resort to it even now when something has really upset me.

One day, when Evie and Daniel were at school, I was listlessly moving around at home, going from room to room without any clear intention, unable to make a decision about what to do from moment to moment. I felt like a lost child.

In the midst of the fog of my sadness, for some reason, I decided to walk to my parents' house. Maybe I had a crazily mistaken notion that my parents might in some way support me if they could see how desperate I felt. As I walked across the grassy playing field of the large park which was on the way to their house, my whole body felt heavy, like it was too much effort to take another step. I had a sudden urge to just stop. I imagined that I could simply lie down on the grass and wait there until someone found me. I imagined that the person who found me might say, "Are you okay?" and I would move my head slowly from side to side to indicate, without having to speak, that actually I wasn't okay. As I continued to walk, I imagined that the person who found me would call an ambulance, or the police, and I might be taken to the local psychiatric hospital for treatment for a nervous breakdown. Maybe Rob would take Evie and Daniel and look after them. I felt in that moment that I had nothing left to give. My children would be better off with Rob than with a bad mother like me. It was an overwhelming desire to surrender, to stop struggling, and let whatever happens happen. I was walking very slowly as I formulated my plan to get off the treadmill of life. I told myself that I would take one more step and then I would lie down. So, I very slowly took one step and stood still for a while. I was afraid to lie down. I told myself that I would do it after the next step. I took another slow step and again stood still. I didn't know if I had the courage to just give up and hope that somebody would help me, and I felt that I didn't have the wherewithal to continue walking forward. I carried on doing this for some time, one footstep forward followed by a long pause, until I realised that I was nearly at the edge of the playing field and getting near to my parents' house. I didn't lie down. I continued walking, and I found myself ringing my parents' doorbell.

My father answered the door. He could see something was wrong.

"Your mum's upstairs," he said, as he went to put the kettle on to make a cup of tea for us.

My father and I took our tea into the lounge, and he asked me if I was alright. Although I had never been inclined to share any of my thoughts or feelings with my parents, either as a child or as an adult, I decided to tell my father a little about how I felt.

"Dad, I just feel like I've had enough. I'm so tired. It's really hard being a single parent. I sometimes think that I'm a rubbish mum. I feel sorry for Evie and Daniel. I don't wish I was still with Rob, but I'm sad that Ravi and I split up."

Just as I spoke, my mother walked into the room.

"What's wrong with you?" she asked. It didn't feel like a kind enquiry, more of an accusation. She didn't sit down, but remained standing near the door. I could tell that she'd been drinking. I could feel a well of tears beginning to spring in my eyes as I repeated what I'd just told my father.

"Well…it's your own fault for making a mess of your marriage, isn't it?" my mother said.

"You chose to get divorced. And as for that stupid Indian boyfriend of yours – it's no wonder he doesn't want you – you couldn't even have children without fertility treatment!"

I was stunned by this verbal attack from my mother.

"Mum…!" I wailed. I couldn't hold back the tears then. I felt like a small child crying for my mother.

"There's no point in you crying, is there?" my mother said, before she walked out of the room. And she was right – there really was no point in crying, in asking for any kind of emotional support from my mother.

"Come on Maeve, no need to be like that," my father said, a weak little protest at my mother's outburst, trying as always to broker peace.

I wiped my eyes and picked up my handbag, said goodbye to my father, and walked out of the house, vowing that I would never again expose my vulnerability to either of them.

Whilst walking home, I decided that I needed to get some help from somewhere to cope with what I was beginning to realise was actually depression rearing its miserable head again. When I got home, I still had a little bit of time before I would need to collect Evie and Daniel from school, so I phoned my GP practice and made an appointment to see my doctor. When I saw him and explained how I felt unable to cope, he prescribed antidepressants. After a couple of weeks of taking the tablets, I started to notice tiny changes in how I felt. I had a little bit more energy. I was more able to make simple decisions, such as what to buy in the supermarket, or what to cook for dinner. Again, as per my usual pattern, I decided to look for another job. Every time I went into work at the GP practice, I was reminded of the abortion, as I had been working there when the abortion happened, and some of my colleagues there knew about it. I wanted to cut any connections with it. I applied for a job as a Health Advisor in the Sexual Health Clinic at the local hospital, and I was delighted when I was offered an interview.

On the weekend before my interview was due, I had arranged to go to a small workshop on women and sexuality which was being held at my friend Annabelle's house. My father had asked if he could borrow my car for the day, because his own car had been stolen. We arranged that I would pick him up and he would drop me to the workshop so he could use my car. When I went into my parents' house to collect my father, I could sense the tension as soon as I walked in the door. My father looked exhausted and miserable.

"Have you had a bad night, Dad?" I asked, quietly.

"Your mum caused a scene in the pub last night, and then she fell over in the street on the way home," he whispered. "I've been awake all night," he sighed. He had to whisper, in case my mother heard him telling me this.

I put an arm around his shoulder.

"Let's go," I said as I gave him the keys to my car.

"You'd better say hello to your mum, otherwise I'll pay for it later," my father said.

I reluctantly walked up the stairs to find my mother putting her make up on in front of the bathroom mirror. She didn't look at me.

"Hello," I grunted, not really wanting to even give her the time of day.

She grunted back. And I turned and walked away. I was so angry with her for upsetting my father, and I had nothing to say. I didn't know in that moment that this would be the last time I would see my mother alive. I imagine that I might have acted differently towards her if I had known – maybe I'd have been a little more kind.

After the workshop, my father had picked me up and I was driving him home. He seemed so sad and was unusually quiet. I asked him if he would like to stop somewhere on the way home for a coffee and a chat. He agreed, so we went to a local pub and sat in the garden, drinking our coffee.

"I don't know, Jacqueline," he said. "When is all this trouble with your mum ever going to stop?"

"I think it will only stop on the day that mum dies," I replied, not knowing how prophetic my words were.

When we got back to the house, I didn't want to go in, because I was angry with my mother. I had learned that it was easier for me to avoid her when I was angry, as any confrontations with me about her drinking and her behaviour seemed to make things worse, especially for my father.

I parked the car outside the house and waited as I watched my father put his key in the lock on the door, to make sure he got in okay. He opened the door and stopped abruptly, then turned and beckoned me in with a slow wave.

I went into the house and saw my mother lying face down at the foot of the stairs, with a halo of blood around her head. Her head was under the telephone table and her body and legs were on the stairs. She was not moving, and I could see that she was not breathing. My father watched as I tried to move her head slightly, and I saw that there was no life in her eyes. There was a very large gaping wound on her forehead. I realised that she was dead. I could see from the waxy colour and coldness of her skin that it was too late to attempt resuscitation. I dialled 999 and was told that an ambulance was on its way to us. My father asked me to call a priest, so that my mother could be given the last rites.

My father and I sat in the sitting room whilst the ambulance crew dealt with my mother's body. We were silent, both of us shocked and stunned. Although there was a part of me which actually didn't feel shocked at all, in spite of witnessing this awful scene.

"So, this is how it ends," I thought.

I had been expecting and preparing myself for some sort of disaster relating to my mother for years. So now it had happened. And I felt a small flicker of relief when I thought to myself, *"Thank God it wasn't my dad."* I had for many years been fearful that my mother might murder him.

I made a cup of tea for my father and started the difficult process of phoning the family to let them know that my mother had died. Family members began to arrive at the house, so I went home to wait for Rob to drop Evie and Daniel back so that I could take them back with me to my parent's house.

That night, in the quiet of my parent's spare bedroom, I decided without much thought that I would contact Ravi to tell him that my mother had died. It's not as though he had any particular relationship with her, there was certainly no closeness between them. I think really it was just an excuse to contact him.

Ravi came to my mother's funeral, but arrived separately, as I was in the funeral car with my family. I sat at the front of the church, looking back at the door so I could spot him coming in and get him to join me. When I saw him, I beckoned to him, but he remained standing at the back of the church. I remember thinking resentfully at the time that he couldn't even be there for me properly on such a difficult occasion, but I also recognised that he was probably just trying to be polite and not intrude on my family. This was after having been in some kind of relationship with him for seven years – he still didn't see himself as in any way part of my family. He always preferred to remain on the periphery.

After the funeral, my sister and her husband stayed with my father, and I went home with Evie and Daniel, having arranged that Ravi would meet us there. After the twins had gone to bed, Ravi and I had a conversation about whether we might get back together. Although I continued to feel very sad about the abortion, I still felt drawn to Ravi and I knew that I loved him. I had not met anyone else in whom I was remotely interested during the time we were apart. I'd had a lot of time to think, during which I had tried to understand why Ravi had reacted the way he did to my pregnancy. I felt that his reaction had been based entirely in fear, and not malice. I decided that I wanted to make a sincere attempt to forgive him for his rejection of me and my unborn child and try to put it behind us, so that we could try to be together again.

I have long been fascinated by the concept of forgiveness, and I believe that forgiveness is not something that you feel – rather it is a choice which we can decide to make or not to make. When we choose to forgive a person who has hurt us, it doesn't mean that we are condoning their behaviour, but we are trying to view what happened with compassion for their failures or mistakes. I knew that hanging on to my anger would harm me, but I also knew that if I chose to forgive Ravi, it would be a decision which I would have to make over and over again every time the pain of the past surfaced in my consciousness like a spectre.

22

Let's Go Round Again

(Average White Band 1980)

So, very tentatively, Ravi and I began to reconnect and to resurrect our relationship. In the weeks between my mother's death and her funeral, I'd had my interview and been offered the job in the Sexual Health Clinic, and for a while I was excited by the novelty of my new role. For a few weeks, I had a renewed sense of joy and huge relief that Ravi and I were back together. I couldn't wait to see him each time, and sex was still powerful and wonderful.

The combination of the excitement of my new job and my reconnection with Ravi provided a distraction which meant that I didn't think very often about the recent death of my mother. My father and I had to attend an inquest into her death, where it was confirmed that blood samples for toxicology at post mortem showed very high levels of alcohol. The verdict of the coroner was that it was an accidental death caused by a head injury, sustained by falling down the stairs whilst under the influence of alcohol. In those early days after her death, the feeling which I can most clearly recollect about the loss of my mother is a sense of relief that all of the traumatic drama and distress associated with her alcoholism had suddenly stopped. Life felt peaceful, as though some fearful shadow had been lifted. I had spent years living on tenterhooks, always on alert that I might receive a call to say that some disaster had occurred involving my mother. Every family event had been ruined by her disruptive behaviour. I was enjoying spending more time with my father, supporting him in his bereavement, getting to know him more closely. Although my father genuinely grieved about the death of his wife, I could see that he too was beginning to breathe a little more easily without the daily drama of living with an alcoholic. I sometimes felt guilty that I didn't seem to be struck by enormous grief about the loss of my mother at the time, particularly as her death had been sudden and traumatic. I thought that it wasn't normal to be so seemingly unaffected by it. In retrospect I can now understand that when my mother died, I was still so deeply mired in grief about the abortion that the loss of my mother almost didn't register with me. It wasn't until many years later that I was really able to acknowledge what the loss of my mother in the context of our very disconnected relationship has meant to me.

My friends were dismayed when I told them that Ravi and I were seeing each other again, but I decided that I had to make my own choices, even if I risked the disapproval of others. However, it wasn't long before the same old problems started to arise between us, the game of me asking when Ravi would make a decision about committing to me, and him saying he wasn't ready yet. This time, although I was still pushing him to make a decision about commitment, I was also aware of some ambivalence of my own, because being with him was also bringing up traumatic memories again about the abortion. I still couldn't really understand why he had been so resolutely unsupportive of me when I was pregnant, especially as, from my perspective at least, it wasn't an unplanned pregnancy. He wouldn't talk to me about what he thought or how he felt, so the reasons behind his complete lack of empathy when I was so vulnerable and distressed remained a mystery to me. I kept thinking that if he had really loved me, the strength of his love would have helped him to put his own fears aside and enabled him to do the right thing. If anyone had asked me then, or even if they were to ask me now, I would still have said that I do believe that he loved me, although to be honest I don't think I could quantify the reasons for my certainty.

I still enjoyed sex with Ravi, but I felt, to some extent, disconnected from my own body and any sense of myself as a woman. I loved Ravi, but I felt angry with him. I looked at his beautiful hands and all I could think about again was what the baby's hands would have looked like. Every time I saw a baby, especially an Indian baby, I felt sick to my stomach. I couldn't share my thoughts with my friends, as I didn't want to hear them telling me to get out of the relationship. I knew they couldn't understand how on earth I could have got back with him after what had happened. Sometimes I would experience moments of what seemed like clarity, when I knew that really there was no way the relationship could ever work, and so I would again tell Ravi that it was over. The shadowy ghost of the lost baby would always haunt me. I would never be free from the deep sadness of loss. Then I would miss Ravi, and one of us would make contact and start the whole cycle all over again. We cycled like this, on and off, with me again sending long letters to Ravi, and him backing off more and more. This constant background of emotional unsettlement in our relationship took a lot of my focus and energy. I was sick of it. I wanted something to change but I didn't know how to make it happen. I just didn't seem to be able to let go of Ravi, and even I could see now how being in such an unhealthy relationship was harming me, and indirectly probably harming Evie and Dan because I was constantly distracted and unhappy.

I could feel myself sliding back into depression yet again. At work, I was once more noticing that I found it difficult to fully engage with the patients whom I was supposed to be helping in the sexual health clinic. Many of the patients were very upset, fearful and angry about having a sexually transmitted infection. Normally, I was very skilled and comfortable at developing a rapport with the patients, which enabled them to trust me enough to be able to share openly with me about their most intimate feelings. Now, when I was in the consulting room all day with patient after patient, trying to help them to reframe and cope with their difficult experiences, I used to try to visualise that I had an invisible protective shield around me, so that I wouldn't absorb their negative energies. I seemed to be once again losing my capacity for empathy. Often, I would see patients who had an unplanned pregnancy and my job was to counsel them to help in the decision-making process about whether to continue or terminate the pregnancy. I found these conversations very uncomfortable, and had to work quite hard to suppress my discomfort in order to remain professionally neutral in my approach.

I was frequently tearful. Each morning when I was on my way to work, I would park my car near the hospital, then hope I wouldn't meet anyone I knew because I was crying as I walked along the road to the clinic. When I arrived at the entrance to the clinic, I used to stand outside for a while, taking deep breaths as I tried to stem the flow of tears, wiping the mascara runs from under my eyes before I went in, preparing myself to pretend to be normal as I greeted my colleagues.

On one occasion at work, I had a disagreement with the

department manager, as she had singled me out for criticism for taking an emergency leave day to take Evie to the doctors. Evie had developed a rash on her back which I suspected, correctly as it turned out, might be shingles, and she was in a lot of pain. Hospital employees were entitled to take up to five emergency leave days per year, and I had never needed to use one of these days, unlike some of my colleagues, who frequently made the most of this leave entitlement. When I went in to the manager's office to discuss this issue and try to defend myself, she told me that I was a very negative person and that I was upsetting all the other staff. She said that I was like a rotten piece of fruit contaminating all the other fruit in the bowl. I was absolutely mortified. I believed I had good relationships with my colleagues and I had never sensed that they had a problem with me. As an inveterate people-pleaser, this hit the very core of my rather shaky sense of self-worth. I spoke with my colleagues and they seemed shocked at what the manager had said to me. They all reassured me that I had not upset them in any way. Some of them told me that they could see that I was often sad, but that they understood this as being completely understandable, because my mother had only recently died.

Although I was very upset about this experience, I reflected on it, and I had to acknowledge that it was quite possible that the negative energy of the sadness and grief which I carried might be having an impact on the people around me. I was aware that I had very little energy or enthusiasm to do anything with Evie and Daniel other than make sure they were fed, had clean clothes and were taken to and from school. Although in retrospect I realise that what I had actually experienced was bullying by the manager, and I should perhaps have taken the matter to the HR department at the hospital, I decided to view being equated to a rotten piece of fruit by my manager as a kick up the backside for me. I had to do something to get out of this chasm of grief.

I was reading a magazine one day when I saw an advert for a three-day coaching event in London. It was being held by an organisation called the Landmark Forum, and the advert claimed that attending the event would bring about shifts in the quality of your life, by creating power, freedom, full self-expression and peace of mind. I was so desperate by that point that I was prepared to try anything, so I applied for a place on the course, paid the fee and arranged for Cissie to look after Evie and Daniel for the three days.

I turned up at the Landmark Forum event with a buzz of excitement, thinking that finally I was doing something radically different in an attempt to bring about change in my life. There were hundreds of people in the audience, listening for hour after hour to the motivational speakers on the stage who were hyping up the huge energy in the auditorium. I remember there being a lot of psychobabble and new terminology for human behavioural patterns, but it was interesting, and I could relate to much of what the speakers were saying, especially about how we can mistakenly allow ourselves to think that we are powerless.

I really couldn't understand why I didn't seem able to disconnect from Ravi, and why I had been so powerless in allowing myself to be coerced into terminating a pregnancy that was so very much wanted and precious to me. I had always seen myself in many ways as a strong and resourceful woman. I'd had enough courage to end a dead marriage, I was independent enough to cope as a single parent of twins with very little support from anyone, either financially or practically, and I'd been intelligent enough to progress quickly into senior positions as a nurse. Yet with Ravi I behaved as though I was absolutely weak and spineless.

On the first evening of the course, we were asked to complete some homework, which was to write a letter to someone with whom we had an unresolved relationship issue. The idea was not that we would necessarily give the letter to the person concerned, rather that it would help to clarify our feelings. Of course, I decided to write a letter to Ravi, and I wrote a very long missive telling him how I felt about everything that had happened between us.

The next morning, once all of the delegates on the course had reconvened in the auditorium, the course leader bounced onto the stage, greeting us all very energetically through his microphone, and asked excitedly if anyone would be prepared to come up to the stage and share their letter with everyone. Without any hesitation, I put my hand up. I had an instant thought that, as I was there and as I didn't know anyone else present, I might as well immerse myself and make the most of this experience. My heart skipped a beat when I was chosen from the audience, but feeling full of bravado, I made my way up to the stage clutching my letter to Ravi in my slippery palms, and I took my place behind the podium microphone. Without mentioning Ravi's name, I read out my letter to the hundreds of people in the audience. It seemed to take forever, but then it was a very long letter.

After I'd finished reading out the letter, I received a loud round of applause from the audience, and then the course leader invited me to take a seat beside him, so that he could try some coaching with me. He started by firing a startling question.

"So, do you really want to be with this zombie?" he asked.

I was taken aback by his use of terminology, and I immediately felt defensive of Ravi.

"He's not a zombie…but...yes, I do want to be with him," I replied, by now having already completely forgotten that I was having this coaching conversation in front of hundreds of people.

"So, what do you want to happen?" asked the course leader.

"I want us to make a positive and wholehearted

commitment to each other. I still love him, and I want to be able to forgive him for the ways in which he has hurt me, especially the abortion. I don't want to hang on to the pain of it all anymore," I replied. "I know that he is a good person, and that his fears are not rooted in any malicious intent towards me. He is afraid of commitment, but I believe that my love can help him to overcome his fears."

"So, what would that commitment look like to you?" he asked.

After a brief pause, I replied, "I want us to be married."

"So, what are you going to do about it?" he asked.

I thought for a moment, and I realised that, although I had spent years waiting and pleading for Ravi to make a decision about whether he would make a commitment to me, I had never actually given him an ultimatum. I took a deep breath and decided that the time had come for me to be clear.

"I'm going to ask him to marry me," I said.

"And what are you going to do if his answer is 'maybe'?" the coach said. "Because 'maybe' is actually a 'no'. Did you realise that? Has it occurred to you that for all of the years you have been together, he has actually been saying 'no' to you?" I had never thought of it like that, but I suddenly understood that this was in fact true.

That afternoon, I phoned Ravi and told him that I was going to come to his apartment the following day. I knew that he would not be at work on a Tuesday, and I too had the day off. I told him that I had one question to ask him, and that I wanted a straight answer to the question, a 'yes' or 'no', and that 'maybe' was not an option. Ravi was angry that I had disturbed him at work. I wouldn't tell him what the question was, and we didn't have time to chat as he was busy at work, but I could tell that he wasn't happy with the direct manner of my announcement.

The next day, after I had dropped Evie and Daniel off at school, I drove to Ravi's. When he opened the door to me, he looked anxious and unhappy. I gave him a hug, which he accepted but didn't return, and I took hold of his hand, leading him over to the sofa.

"Ok, I'm not going to beat around the bush," I said. "I have a question to ask you."

A silent pause, whilst Ravi looked at me, waiting for me to tell him what this was all about.

I took both of his hands in mine and looked him straight in the eye. I was nervous but still pumped up with resolve and adrenaline after the Landmark Forum experience, that once and for all I was going to one way or another put an end to the impasse between us.

My mouth was dry as I asked, "Will you marry me?"

I waited for Ravi to respond. He looked away from me and removed his hands from my clasp.

"Umm…I don't know…probably one day we'll get married, but I'm not ready yet…I have things to think about and to sort out before I can make a decision about that," Ravi replied. "I don't like it that you are putting me under pressure."

"Ravi, I know I'm putting you under pressure now, but I am tired of waiting. I'm tired of being kept in the corner of your life, like some dirty secret, even after all these years. I don't want to live like that anymore," I said.

I was disappointed, but not shocked, by Ravi's response. I had promised myself that if the answer was yet again another 'maybe', I would take that as a 'no', and I would end this painful situation once and for all.

"Ok Ravi, what you're saying to me is that maybe we will get married in the future. Did you know that 'maybe' is actually a 'no'? And that in reality you have been saying no to me for years?" I asked.

I stood up from the couch, took a deep breath, and tried to suppress the prickling of tears which was stinging my eyes.

"Before I came here today, I told myself that if you responded with a maybe, then I would end our relationship once and for all," I said, quite calmly, concealing the fear and panic staring to ascend inside me. "So, Ravi, I'm going to go home now and I want you to know that it's over…and this time I really mean it. I love you, with all of my heart, and I will always love you, but it's over."

I turned away from him, picked up my handbag and walked over to the door without looking back at him. Just as

I opened the door, Ravi spoke. "Please don't go," he said, his voice shaking. I turned to look at him and could see that his eyes were full of tears. I didn't know what to do then, so I remained standing at the door, still gripping the door handle.

"Come here…please," Ravi said.

I walked back over to him and sat next to him on the sofa. I didn't speak.

"I do want to marry you," said Ravi.

I still didn't speak.

"I was just surprised by you coming down here and demanding an answer the way you did. You put me on the spot."

I immediately retreated into guilt mode, knowing that I'd made him feel uncomfortable, so I apologised for upsetting him.

I put my arms around him and we hugged for a minute. I was trying to work out what to say. I didn't know what to do.

"Do you mean it?" I asked him.

"Yes."

"So, we are going to get married?" I asked, not quite believing it.

"Yes," Ravi replied, with his characteristic lack of verbal embellishment.

We got into bed and made love as usual. I was quietly excited and wanted to talk about where and when we would get married, but I knew the drill – keep quiet and don't ask too many questions.

I drove home, feeling quite unsettled. Technically, Ravi had said yes to my proposal, so apparently that meant that we were going to get married. But his acceptance was given to me reluctantly, and I knew in my heart that it was not a genuine yes. Later that day I tried to draw him into conversation on the phone about what had transpired that morning. He was quiet. I told Ravi that I had shared with my father the news about our agreement to marry, albeit tentatively, like I was testing the water. Ravi was annoyed with me for having mentioned anything to my father. This was when the warning bells which had been giving little chimes began to ring loudly and clearly. If things were really as they should be, I thought that I should have been able to shout from the rooftops with excitement about our apparent decision to get married. I knew in my heart that Ravi had reluctantly accepted my proposal because he didn't want me to leave him or to end our relationship, but in reality, he was no more certain about making a commitment to me than he had ever been.

It took a further three days for me to get up the courage to tell Ravi again that it was over. I asked him not to contact me again and resolved to get on with my life without him.

23

Never Can Say Goodbye

(Gloria Gaynor 1975)

Shortly after this episode, I was at work one day when I developed a severe headache. It felt like a knife boring into my left eye. The pain was relentless. I had to leave work early, because I could hardly speak and couldn't concentrate on anything. I spent the rest of the day in bed with the curtains drawn, and when I got up the next morning to take the twins to school it felt like the worst hangover I'd ever had. The pain returned again by the evening and I spent a very restless night, unable to sleep, as the paracetamol I'd taken had absolutely no effect. I phoned work to tell them that I would need to take the day off sick and I made an appointment to see my GP later in the day.

My GP was concerned about the sudden onset of the headache and the severity of it, so he arranged for me to have an urgent MRI scan. I had the scan the following day, the result of which was normal. I saw my GP again, who suggested that the headache was migraine, and he prescribed a drug for me to take if the pain occurred again. Over the next few weeks, I had repeated episodes of migraine and was becoming increasingly exhausted, as I wasn't sleeping well. I was continuing to go to work despite the fact that I seemed to have very little emotional or physical reserves left.

By now, Evie and Daniel were teenagers. One weekend, Daniel was getting ready to go to his Saturday job, which was at a warehouse approximately ten-minutes walking distance from our home. The weather was dreadful, a heavy storm was raging and it was raining torrentially. Normally Daniel walked to work, but I considered offering him a lift because it was raining so heavily. I sat on the sofa, looking at the rain pelting the windows and watching Daniel put his coat on, and I did not have the wherewithal to speak. I had ground to a halt. Daniel didn't ask me for a lift. I think he knew that I had reached a very low point, and being the sensitive and kind young person that he is, he didn't want to ask anything of me. I watched Daniel walk out into the rain, hunched over like a question mark as he walked past the house trying to avoid being completely soaked, and I felt that I was the worst mother in the world because I hadn't offered him a lift, but I couldn't seem to make myself move. It was in that rock bottom moment that I knew that my depression had reached the point where I couldn't ignore it anymore.

I went back to my GP and asked him to prescribe

antidepressants again and to refer me for counselling. He agreed to do both, and suggested that I should take some time away from work. He gave me a sickness certificate, citing depression, for me to give to my employer. I felt a little embarrassed to think that my manager and colleagues would know that I was having mental health problems, but I was too much in need of help to worry about it.

I remember feeling as though I had been treading water endlessly in a turbulent sea, for a very long time, buffeted around by rough waves. I was utterly exhausted from trying to keep myself afloat, and now I had given up the struggle and allowed myself to sink to the bottom of the sea. Instead of fear I now felt a strange peace as I floated around down there on the sea bed. I had surrendered, and the world hadn't fallen apart. I spent the next month mostly sleeping. I would get up and take the twins to school, then go back home and sleep until I had to pick them up later. I used to put headphones on and listen to soothing music to try to make myself feel calmer. There was one song in particular called 'The Deep', by Lucinda Drayton, which I used to listen to over and over again for hours because the lyrics seemed to capture so perfectly how I felt. After around four weeks of this restorative rest, I started to notice that on some days I was actually still awake by nine pm, instead of needing to crash out as soon as the twins were in bed.

My appointment came through with the counsellor, and

as I slowly began to share my story with her, I was able to acknowledge the weight of the boulder of unprocessed grief which I had been carrying around on my shoulders for years, a huge sack, stuffed full of the pain about being sexually abused as a teenager, the experience of infertility, a failed marriage, the loss of a much wanted baby through a forced abortion, being kept hidden in the corner of Ravi's world for so many years, the lack of connection to my mother and the years of trauma caused by her alcoholism, and then her sudden death. The counsellor helped me to understand the relationship between my parents and me a little better. As part of my story, I have shared with you about times when I felt badly let down by my parents, but I want you to know that when I think about my mother and father, I think of them overwhelmingly with love and compassion. There is no such thing as a perfect parent, myself included. My parents got many important things right – they taught me how to be kind, how to give generously and to always be hospitable to any guest in my home. My mother was a fantastic cook and she fed her family well, regardless of how much she may have had to drink at times. My parents were very sociable people, very often inviting large groups of friends and family to our house, so I have great memories of our home being filled with the lively sounds of happy people laughing together and singing along to many familiar Irish songs. Our home was warm, comfortable and clean, and I was always welcome to bring my friends into the house. My mother was a very attractive and sexy blonde, who was much admired by many of my male school friends, which made me feel proud of her, rather than jealous. My mother could be playful, sometimes almost childlike, and these were the times I remember best. My parents never once hit me or my brother and sister, I don't remember them ever shouting at us or arguing in front of us when we were children. I remember sensing that they loved each other and I witnessed affection between them. My father was a very kind man who taught me to know that I was no less important and no more important than any other person on the planet. He was clever and funny, and would chat to anyone he met, strangers included, in a way which always left them feeling uplifted. Both of my parents came from very large families – contraception being absolutely forbidden for their devout Irish Catholic parents. Their own mothers and fathers would have been just-about surviving, trying to provide for their huge broods with very little money and living in extremely small homes. Both of my grandmothers would have spent most of their adult lives being almost continuously pregnant whilst having to care for their numerous existing children, with none of today's benefits of disposable nappies and washing machines. So, I imagine that my parents would not have experienced much individual cosseting and attention when they were children, and perhaps they never learned that this too is important for a child. My mother and father would not have been wallowing around in the world of emotions in the way that our generations can sometimes do. I am grateful to both of my parents, both of whom are now deceased, for all that they taught me, including sometimes through adversity, and I think of them both with love. I used to wish that I had the sort of mother who I thought was "normal", and sometimes I do still think that this would have been nice, but I genuinely believe that sometimes it's the difficult things which shape us and can teach us the most. The powerful gifts my mother gave me were that, through her, I learned how to love unconditionally, how to feel compassion rather than judgement, and to be able to truly forgive. I have used these gifts many times in my adult life. I never hold grudges against anyone and will always try to understand that mostly, when a person is behaving hurtfully, it because they are actually hurting in some way themselves.

During the counselling process, I began to understand on a deeper level how my insecure attachment to my mother, and to some extent my father too, had led me to develop a deep-seated insecurity in how I related to others as an adult. I hadn't ever consciously thought of myself as being an insecure person, but I could see how my early life experiences had led to my people-pleasing behaviour, how I would go to enormous lengths to avoid disapproval in any shape or form. I began to understand how striving for perfection, trying never to make a mistake or put a foot wrong in order to avoid rejection or criticism, was actually very unhealthy and unhelpful as a mode of being.

Around this time, a friend from work, Theresa, came to visit me at home whilst I was off sick from work. She expressed concern for me and acknowledged my grief about the abortion. She was a devout Catholic, and she asked me if I would like to accompany her to a special mass which was to be held in a local Catholic church for women who had lost a baby, whether it was from a miscarriage, a stillbirth, or an abortion. I agreed to join her at the mass. There was a larger congregation than I had expected – mostly women and just a few men. The priest gave a beautiful sermon during which he acknowledged the grief which a woman might experience after the loss of a baby, regardless of the manner in which that baby was lost. There was no tone of judgement, just an expression of compassion for any woman who was suffering. There was a life-sized statue of the Virgin Mary near the altar, and we were invited to go up to the altar, to take a tea-light candle and light it from a large candle which was near the statue. We were asked to bring the name of the baby to mind as we lit the candle, if we knew it, or to think of a name for the baby even if the baby had never been born or we didn't know the sex of the lost child. We could then place the lit candle at the feet of the statue of Mary and leave it there burning for the rest of the duration of the mass. At the end, we could either collect our tea-light and take it home with us or leave it where it was. I had no way of knowing whether my baby was a boy or a girl, so I decided to imagine that it may have been a boy, and I gave him the name Matthew, as I knew that the meaning of this name was 'gift from God'. I chose to leave the candle where it was after the mass was finished as a symbolic gesture of letting go. There was something very powerful about this ritual which did create for the first time a small glimpse of peace in my heart.

I told the counsellor about my experience at the mass. She explored with me about how the act of creating a symbolic ritual had helped me to shift a little from my place of despair. I acknowledged that it was something about being able to take some kind of action, rather than remaining stuck and helplessly paralysed by grief. The counsellor then suggested another ritual which might be of help. I was to buy some helium balloons, each one to represent something which I wished to let go of, and go out somewhere in nature where I could be completely alone. I was to let the balloons float into the sky whilst I said goodbye to each thing or person that I wanted to release my painful emotional attachment to. So, ignoring the slight feeling of discomfort that what I was planning to do wasn't very eco-friendly, I bought three balloons, each a different colour, and wrote three letters to the people I wished to release my attachments to. One was for my mother, one was for my lost baby, and one was for Ravi.

On a sunny day, I drove out to a place in the countryside

where I knew I wouldn't be likely to meet anyone. I walked a long way across the fields carrying the three balloons in a tight grip as they bounced in the air behind me. Although, as far as I was aware, nobody could see me, I felt quite self-conscious that if anyone did see me, they would probably wonder what on earth I was up to. Eventually I found a nice secluded area at the edge of a field and I sat down on the warm grass. First, I read out loud the letter saying goodbye to my mother, and then I let the first balloon go. I watched calmly as the balloon floated up. I waited for a couple of minutes and then I started to read the letter to my lost baby. This was more difficult – it was a letter so full of pain and regret. I finished reading the letter haltingly and I felt reluctant to let go of the second balloon. When I eventually let it go, I sat down on the grass and watched it float high into the sky with an overwhelming feeling of sadness, and I cried silent tears. After a few minutes just sitting there, I read the letter to Ravi. This was easier, but once I had let the third balloon go, I watched intensely as it drifted further and further away, high in the sky, until I saw the last tiny speck of it completely vanish from my sight and I suddenly felt a strange sense of panic, an internal voice crying *"No!"* I didn't want to lose sight of the balloon – I was so resistant to letting go of my attachment to Ravi. But, immediately after this unexpected feeling of panic, suddenly I actually experienced a huge internal emotional shift, that I had finally let go of Ravi and to any ideas of a future with him. It seemed quite crazy to me, after all it wasn't actually Ravi that I had just released into the ether, it was just a balloon, but the ritualistic action of what I had just done was signalling something very firmly to my subconscious mind about my intention to move on.

24

Respect Yourself

(The Staple Singers 1971)

I think of that day as a turning point for me, as during the following weeks I could sense the rippling excitement of recovery within me. There was a feeling that I'd been like a chrysalis for a very long time, and now the chrysalis was cracking open. Long forgotten feelings of optimism were stirring my butterfly wings and a new life was imminent, full of possibilities. I started to feel a desire to socialise, to meet old friends and make new ones. I was back at work, and once again enjoying being able to see myself as the skilled and competent nurse that I was, instead of the burnt-out failure I'd being feeling for such a long time.

I no longer needed childcare to be able to go out in the evenings, as Evie and Daniel were now old enough to be left unsupervised at home. As I started to accept invitations to social events, an interesting new dynamic developed where it was almost as though my children and I had swapped roles, like I was the excitable teenager and they were the parents wanting to know what time I would be home. They had got used to me always being at home, a quiet presence in their lives, and weren't quite sure what to make of this different gregarious mother. They were especially concerned when I announced my intentions to get a tattoo! It was something which I had never previously considered, but for some reason the idea of it now appealed to me. Maybe it was something about living life without fear and to its maximum possible fullness. A need to experience everything with an open heart and make whatever decisions I wanted to about my own life and my own body without having to seek approval from anyone else. On reflection, it really was like belatedly experiencing being the rebellious teenager that I'd never allowed myself to be.

I decided that I would like to have a very small tattoo of a butterfly on my lower abdomen, a place where only I, or any future lovers, would see it – or perhaps medical professionals if ever I was being examined. The symbolism of the butterfly was connected to Ravi and the painting I had created for him, and to my new sense of emerging from the chrysalis. I wanted to make a permanent mark on my body as a memory of the happy times Ravi and I had shared, a reminder of the all the good things and not the sad things. It's a little ironic that the act of getting a permanent tattoo linked to remembrance of Ravi was also a symbol of my letting go of him.

I bounced into the tattoo parlour, full of excitement and bravado. I explained to the young male tattoo artist that I wanted a tiny blue butterfly tattoo and that I would like it on the left side of my lower abdomen. He then asked me to stand up and show him where I wanted it. I stood up, facing towards him, and pulled down the front of my jeans and my underwear. Suddenly, I felt very uncomfortable as I exposed my saggy and stretch-marked tummy to this young man. I blushed with embarrassment as I wondered what he might have been thinking, how he might have judged me to be a silly old woman who was being quite ridiculous because I wanted a tattoo. I could feel him applying some local anaesthetic cream and a waterproof dressing to the chosen spot on my abdomen, and then he asked me to wait in the waiting room for fifteen minutes to give the anaesthetic cream time to start working.

As I sat in the waiting room, I continued to berate myself with a barrage of fearful thoughts. I imaged how the tattooist was probably wondering how anyone could possibly think that it was a good idea to place a beautiful tattoo, a little piece of permanent art, on a tummy which was now so obviously very far removed from being the tanned and toned abdomen of my youth. I looked at the door and considered that I could just walk out and forget the idea of having a tattoo. I had already paid, so I wouldn't have to explain my sudden change of plan. I told myself that it was my body anyway, so I didn't have to explain anything to them. As I had this empowering thought about my body, I had a sudden flash of awareness that yes, actually it was MY body I and I could do whatever I liked. And if I wanted to have a little tattoo, then it really didn't matter what my tummy looked like or what anyone thought about it. I placed my hands on my curvy abdomen and I thought about how this part of my body was actually the home of my twins, the place where they grew inside me like a miracle, and the internal narrative immediately changed – reminding me that this part of my body was truly a very precious part of me. I couldn't think of any other part of me which deserved more to be adorned with a beautiful butterfly. Now, whenever I look at my lovely little secret tattoo, it reminds me of the very valuable lesson it taught me about self-acceptance on that day.

My sister Sinead persuaded me to go out with her one evening to a local Irish social club. After having a few drinks, I began to relax and I even agreed to join Sinead on the dance floor. It had been a very long time since I had danced, and it felt good to move my body again, and to laugh with my sister, to loosen up a little more the straightjacket of grief which had been wrapped around me. At one point, I was sitting near the bar, and I noticed a tall and very handsome Asian man looking over in my direction. He smiled at me and I returned his smile, enjoying the thrill of this little flirtation. After a while he came over and we started to chat, sharing a little of our life stories over a couple of drinks. He told me that his name was Ajeet and that he was married but had separated from his wife. He told me that he was temporarily living with one of his male friends. I felt very attracted towards him and could sense that the feeling was mutual. It was the first time I'd ever felt attracted to anyone other than Ravi in many years, and this was exciting to me. *'Maybe there is life after Ravi?'* I thought. Towards the end of the evening, Ajeet asked for my phone number and I gave it to him, not really expecting him to call me. A couple of days later, he contacted me and I accepted his invitation to meet for a drink. We arranged to meet one evening when Evie and Daniel were at Rob's, and whilst we were at the pub I was thrilled and excited to notice the new sensation of sexual chemistry with this stranger. I decided that maybe if I had sex with Ajeet I might at last be able to try to break the bond of sexual faithfulness which I had maintained with Ravi. I imagined that this act would mean that I could never be tempted to reunite with Ravi. I could finally break the never-ending cycle with him.

So, Ajeet and I had sex and I found that I was able to enjoy it and to engage in it fully. We met a few times over the subsequent few weeks, and although I didn't have the feeling that I wanted to be in a serious long-term relationship with him, I enjoyed his company and I felt a new light-heartedness within myself. After a while I began to wonder why Ajeet never answered his phone. My call would always go to his voicemail and he would call me back sometime after. He seemed reluctant to let me know where he lived or to invite me to his place, saying that he and his friend had a rule that they wouldn't bring women back to the house. I began to suspect that he may still be living with his wife, and when I confronted him about this, he confirmed that my suspicions were correct. I felt very uncomfortable that I'd been having sex with him whilst he was still married, and I stopped seeing him, but I did think that my objective about breaking the bond with Ravi had been achieved. It had at least taught me that it was possible for me to feel attracted enough to someone other than Ravi for me to open myself up sexually, and hopefully this meant that in the future I could now imagine the possibility of a proper new relationship.

25

Move On Up

(Curtis Mayfield 1970)

An opportunity arose for me to take a new role as a Practice Nurse in a local GP surgery which would require me to take a lead with developing sexual health services within the practice. The practice had a high number of HIV positive patients, and along with general nursing duties I was to focus on developing care standards for the HIV positive patients, to encourage increased HIV testing amongst the high-risk cohort of patients on the practice list and to increase testing for other sexually transmitted diseases. Having worked in a sexual health clinic for so many years, this post was ideal for me, so I agreed to take the job.

My new job gave me fresh energy, something different to excite me. I felt that I'd at last been able to put some real distance between myself and Ravi, so after a few months I was surprised to find myself yet again being sucked into communication with him after he phoned me to see how I was. I was pleased to hear from him, but the emotional ties had been weakened with the passage of time and as a result of my brief sexual liaison with Ajeet. I agreed to meet Ravi, knowing that it was possible that we might have sex, so just as a precaution I went to a sexual health clinic to have tests for sexually transmitted diseases before I met him again. The test results were all clear. I admitted to Ravi that I'd had sex with someone else, and although he was upset by this revelation, he acknowledged that he didn't really have any right to complain about it. There followed a few weeks where once again we tried to resume our relationship, but my heart wasn't really in it in the same way as it had been before. I did still love him, but something in me had closed off and I wasn't able to ignore the rational voice inside my head telling me that it would never be possible to repair the emotional damage done by my relationship with Ravi, especially his reaction to my pregnancy. I kept thinking that if my reason for making the decision to terminate my pregnancy was because I'd had a split second of clarity that I didn't want to be in any way connected to Ravi in the future, then if we stayed together, it would mean that my baby had died for nothing. It was only a few weeks before I told Ravi, once again, that I really didn't want to be with him anymore. Even though it broke my heart, and I think Ravi's heart, to do this, I told him that I no longer loved him and that I really didn't want him to contact me ever again.

I was full of resolve, with a growing sense of purpose and clarity in my life. I knew that I was a good person, and that I deserved to have a relationship with someone who was able to love me wholeheartedly. I knew that I was no longer willing to tolerate anything less than that, and that I would be better off on my own than in a relationship which harmed me emotionally.

I thought about the example I had been setting to Evie and Daniel about love and relationships. Although at that point they were unaware of what had happened to me about the termination of pregnancy, they had seen me over many years being emotionally distressed and depressed. They had witnessed the failed marriage of their parents, and then spent years observing the ways in which Ravi had failed to be present or to support me. I worried that if they were to model their own future relationships on the examples that I had shown them, they would be on a sure path to unhappiness. Evie might have low expectations for how men should treat her, and Daniel might think that it was okay to be an emotionally distant partner. I didn't know if it would be possible to undo any of the damage which I felt I might have caused to them by my own failures and lack of strength. I had no way of knowing at this point. I started saying yes to every invitation which came my way, and again decided to dip a cautious toe into the world of online dating. I met a few nice men, and had some pleasant dates, but there was nobody whom I was especially interested in.

I picked myself up and started to really think about what I wanted my life to look like. I was single. I was healthy. I had two beautiful children who still needed me to be present to them. I was ready for change. I was in a new emotional space where I could learn and grow. I began to see myself as a free spirit and I did not want to be constrained by anyone. I could stand on my own two feet. I could make my own choices and be free. I had a large group of good friends, both male and female, and I was beholden to nobody. I felt no need to look for love. I felt happy with myself. I was proud of myself for finally standing up and saying what I wanted with real strength and conviction, not hesitancy. I was looking forward to the future, whatever that may hold. By this time, my children were seventeen years old. They enjoyed having me to themselves. I did still think often about the baby with a feeling of longing and sadness. I still found that if I was out in public, I would look at all the people around me and think about how they were all once a fetus, and because their mother gave birth to them, they were here on this planet, walking around and breathing, living their lives. I would look at them and wonder if their mother had ever considered having an abortion, and that if she had, possibly that person sitting in front of me would not be alive, physically existing on this planet. I still find myself having that train of thought when I am in crowded public places.

I would look at Evie and Daniel and feel so grateful for their existence in my life. I would think about the little soul who would have been their brother or sister, and try to imagine what our little family would have been like. How my children might have really loved this little person. I used to make myself engage with other people's babies, trying to feel comfortable again about being in the presence of babies. Trying to feel the pleasure of it and not experiencing it as pain. I got lots of opportunities to hold babies in my work as a practice nurse, and after a while of pretending to myself that I felt okay with being around babies, I began to realise that sometimes I actually did feel okay. I could love babies again. And it didn't always hurt me. I still thought of Ravi, but I did not think of him in such a way that I wanted to see him again. I felt no anger, no hatred, just compassion for him in his weakness and indecision. The wounds of grief were still within me, but the experience of pain was less raw when its presence rippled up into my consciousness, and the scars were finally beginning to heal. I felt well and happy. No more crippling headaches, less tiredness. I had more energy and more interest in the world around me. I wanted to engage with people again, and I didn't need antidepressant medications any more. My butterfly wings were starting to shimmer with movement.

26

At Last

(Etta James 1961)

One of my Practice Nurse colleagues, Heather, asked me to accompany her to a meeting being held by one of the pharmaceutical companies. There was going to be a lecture about the treatment of restless legs.

"No, I don't think I can be bothered," I said. I wasn't at all interested in learning about restless legs.

"Oh…come on…it will be a laugh!... And there's food!" said Heather.

I had always enjoyed the networking aspect of medical education meetings, and I had made a vow to myself to say yes to every invitation, so I decided I would go along to it, as I had nothing else planned.

I was very disappointed when Heather didn't turn up for the meeting, especially as I ended up sitting next to one of the GPs I had always made sure to avoid when I was a drug rep, Dr Oliver Thomson. I had known of Dr Thomson for many years, having seen him at various medical meetings and study events since the early nineties. I had actually worked for a short time in his surgery as a nurse, in the early 90s, as part of a research trial in Primary Care, and perceived him to be a very serious person, in fact quite unfriendly. I hadn't ever spoken to him directly, but he never seemed to smile much. I had never tried to visit him when I was a Medical Sales Representative, as I had imagined that he would be the kind of GP who despised medical reps and who would try to tie them in knots intellectually when discussing prescribing and pharmacology.

And now I found myself sitting next to him. I inwardly cursed Heather for her non-attendance.

The lecture on restless legs was predictably boring. After the lecture, people started chatting around the table.

"So, are you a rep then?" Oliver asked as he turned towards me. "What's your name?"

"No," I said, with a nervous little laugh. "I'm a Practice Nurse. My name is Jacqueline, but most people call me Jackie."

"Ok, Jackie, in that case you can call me Oliver!" he said, with a little chuckle.

Oliver started chatting to me. I told him that I was a single parent of 17-year-old twins. I started burbling on about my rather vague, but long held plan to run off and live in India in an ashram one day in the future, perhaps doing voluntary work there in the field of HIV. I was waiting until Evie and Daniel had left home and they were living independently, then I was going to sell my house and go to India to live a simple life. I said that I would come back to UK to help when grandchildren were born etc, but otherwise, my future life would be in India. I got the feeling that Oliver was quite intrigued by what I was telling him. He seemed interested to know more about the reasons for my Indian dreams.

I don't know why I have always felt this connection with India. I am obsessed with it. I remember even as a young girl I used to write little fictional stories about an Indian boy. I don't know whether or not I believe in the idea of past lives, but if such a thing exists then I think I must have lived in India many lifetimes ago. I sometimes even wonder whether Ravi and I may have been together in a previous lifetime and are trying to work things through during this incarnation. So much of what has happened between us feels compulsive, rather than logical or rational. If I hear even the first few notes of Indian music, I'll suddenly stop whatever I'm doing as it catches my attention in a way that no other music ever has. It feels as though I am instantly recognising something from an unconscious place within me. I am fascinated with the colours and patterns associated with Indian clothing and architectural design. And I love the sultry beauty of burnished brown skin, jet black hair and deep chocolate eyes.

Anyway, back to the story! Oliver talked about his two

children, who were now grown up. He didn't mention his wife, and I noticed that he wasn't wearing a wedding ring, but I assumed he was married and didn't really think about it. As we chatted, I suddenly became aware that I was enjoying his company and I felt surprisingly relaxed, considering how I'd always thought of him as being a bit scary. He was chatty, and funny and open. I noticed his rich warm voice and I loved the sound of it. The atmosphere between us felt a little flirty, and I was enjoying it. At one point I looked at his mouth, his lovely smile and thought to myself, *Would I kiss you?* I felt quite shocked when the answer to my internal question came back as a yes – particularly as I had had such a negative opinion of him previously. And he was nothing like what I'd thought was 'my type', with his silver hair, bright blue eyes and upper middle-class Englishness.

"How come you're here on your own?" Oliver asked.

"Heather, the Practice Nurse at the Melrose Health Centre, was supposed to come with me but she bailed out," I said.

"Oh, I know Heather, she's a friend of mine. She used to be our district nurse!" Oliver said. "Sometimes the two of us meet up for a drink – just as friends."

Then he suggested that perhaps the three of us could meet up for a drink sometime.

I wondered for a moment whether Oliver might actually be asking me out on a date. I did like him, but I really did not want to get involved with him romantically if he was married.

I'd had enough traumatic nightmares already in my life. But I thought maybe if I met him with Heather as a group rather than as a date that would be okay, and perhaps he might be nice to get to know as a friend. So, I gave him my phone number.

The next day, I called Heather to ask why she hadn't turned up to the meeting.

"I sat next to one of your friends, Dr Thomson," I said. "He seems like a really nice person – shame he's married though!" I said, with a laugh.

"Not for much longer," said Heather. "He told me that he is getting divorced."

Heather then proceeded to tell me a little about what Oliver had shared with her about his unhappy marriage.

Later that day, Oliver phoned to ask me to meet him.

"Well, I think you're nice, but you're married, aren't you? I don't want to get involved with you if you're married," I said.

"Yes, I am married, but we live separate lives and we are planning to get divorced," Oliver replied. "We have both been unhappy for years, but we decided to wait until our youngest child, our daughter, has finished her A-levels before we split up, because we don't want to mess up her exams."

It was now March, and his daughter was due to finish her A-levels that summer.

I hesitated briefly, then I agreed to meet him, thinking that

I was prepared to hear a bit more about his marital situation. I had no intention of getting involved with him unless he was telling me the truth about his marriage having already ended.

We went to a local country pub. I felt so strange to be in his company. I'd really had such a negative impression about him previously, and yet here I was sitting in a pub with Dr Thomson listening to the story of his marriage. I found it quite surreal.

Oliver reiterated what he had told me about the plans for divorce. He said that he really liked me and that he would like to see me again. I said that I liked him too, but I did not want to have a secret affair whilst he was still married. I told him that I'd had enough relationship trauma in my life, and as much as I liked him, I was quite happy being by myself and I didn't need the hassle. He told me that, as he and his wife were imminently going to separate, and that they had talked about details such as splitting their financial assets etc, he would tell his wife that he had met me and that she really wouldn't care about it. So, I accepted this and we decided to start seeing each other.

However, far from not being remotely bothered by Oliver starting a relationship with me, his wife reacted with enormous distress and anger. She was terribly upset. I felt absolutely awful and mortified with shame. I met with Oliver and told him that I did not want to see him again, that perhaps his wife did have feelings after all and that he should forget about me and concentrate on finding out whether his marriage was repairable. Oliver was crestfallen at this and became very upset. I was insistent that this was the right thing to do, for everyone concerned. We spent a couple of days without any contact. I felt deflated and disappointed that I had allowed myself to get into this situation. I felt guilty towards his wife. I felt disappointed because I really liked Oliver. Apart from feeling physically attracted to him, I could see that he was a good man. He was open, honest and prepared to talk about his feelings. He seemed to really like me and he was so enthusiastic about telling me so. His affection was given so easily and without restriction. So different from how it had been with Ravi, from whom I'd failed to elicit open warmth, like trying to get blood out of a stone, for so many years. I couldn't understand how I had lived like that. How had I ever thought that was a normal way to live?

The day after I told Oliver that I didn't want to see him again, I had to give a talk at the hospital for a group of trainee GPs, teaching them how to manage sexual health in Primary Care. Oliver was there in his role as a GP Trainer. I felt excruciatingly uncomfortable having to put on a brave professional front and pretend that I didn't even know him, when both of us were struggling with difficult feelings and much embarrassment about our situation.

After the study session had finished, Oliver asked me to meet him at a local pub for a drink, so that we could talk. He said he understood why I had asked to end the relationship, but he wanted me to know that his marriage really was over, despite the unforeseen reaction of his wife. He said that his wife did not love him and he did not love her. Their marriage really had ended long before he had met me and they had agreed to divorce a long time previously. He felt that their marriage was not repairable, and he believed that his wife's reaction to his relationship with me was not motivated by love. He said that he wanted to be with me. He told me that now he had met me he couldn't 'un-meet' me. I was uncertain about what to do, but I did continue to see him from time to time, and very tentatively our relationship began to grow, with the shadow of the breakdown of his marriage hanging over us. Oliver's wife then initiated divorce proceedings, citing his adultery with me as the cause of the breakdown of the marriage. Although I knew in my heart that I had not actually caused the marriage to break down, that the problems between Oliver and his wife and their intention to separate had been there long before I came on the scene, I accepted that Oliver meeting me had probably precipitated the actual separation sooner than it would have happened had we not met.

I look back on those early days of my relationship with Oliver with mixed feelings. I was amazed at how open and honest he was about his affection towards me. He was demonstrative, warm and loving. He continually expressed his joy at having found me. He was absolutely and fearlessly committed to being with me. He was proud of me and couldn't wait to introduce me to all of his friends and family. This was all so completely new to me and so very different to how it had been with Ravi. Whilst all of these wonderful elements of our new relationship were causing me to feel much happiness and excitement, there were also times when I was aware that, in some ways, I wasn't able to let myself relax and accept this love, to allow myself to be cared for and emotionally supported in the way that Oliver loved me. It took quite a long time before I gradually allowed myself to feel safe and to know that I didn't have to be anything other than my whole and true self and I could still be loved. The shadow side of this new love was the uncomfortable guilt and shame I carried, knowing that Oliver's ex-wife was so angry and hurt. As a people-pleaser, I couldn't cope with imagining how much hurt I must have caused this woman whom I'd never met – how she must hate me. I found it difficult to understand why she had reacted the way she did to Oliver's relationship with me when, according to Oliver, they didn't love each other. However, it wasn't up to me to judge how she should or shouldn't feel or react – I had only heard Oliver's side of the story. I did feel some resentment though that I had been made a scapegoat and held unfairly responsible for the demise of their marriage.

Oliver and I had been seeing each other for about six

weeks, when out of the blue, one evening when I was on my own at home, the phone rang and I heard Ravi's voice saying a very tentative "Hello". My mouth went dry and my heart started thumping.

We hadn't spoken for many months, since our final break up. I still thought about Ravi every day, with both sadness and fondness, but I was no longer pining for him. I was enjoying getting to know Oliver, slowly learning to trust him. I was moving on in my life and I was very gradually becoming able to put thoughts about the termination into a box in the back of my mind, where some of its power to hurt me was waning.

"Hi," I said. Then I waited for him to speak.

"I've got something to ask you," said Ravi.

"Ok," I said, not having any idea what he was about to say to me.

"I want to know if you will marry me?" Ravi said.

I was silent.

"I'm ready now. I miss you and I want to be with you. Will you marry me?"

I gasped. Stunned by what he had just said and by the decisive directness of it.

I took a deep breath before I replied, knowing that what I was about to tell him would cause him pain.

"Ravi… I have met someone else."

He was silent.

"I'm sorry, Ravi, but it's too late. I've met someone else,"

I said.

Again, Ravi was silent. I started to fill the silence by telling him a little bit about Oliver. Not saying too much, as I didn't want to hurt Ravi, but just enough to let him know that Oliver and I were in a new relationship. I told him that Oliver was married but was separated and getting divorced, and that I hadn't been the cause of this.

Ravi began to talk, his shaky voice trying to convince me that we were meant to be together. He told me that I would be foolish to continue seeing this married man who had children. Ravi said that I would be better off with him, because he had no ties and could be there for me one hundred percent. He said he could buy a house in my home town and that I could give up work if I wanted to. He said that he could help with supporting Evie and Daniel through university, including financially. He said that I wouldn't have to worry about money any more. We could travel the world, see the Taj Mahal, and we'd have our honeymoon in Kerala. He asked me how I could give up on him after we had been through so much together and because we knew each other so well. I was absolutely stunned by this turnaround. I didn't know what to say – I just listened, so Ravi began to fill the silence by asking me if we could meet up to talk. I agreed to meet him, so we arranged that he would come to my house the next day.

I told Oliver about the phone call and that I had agreed to meet Ravi. Oliver was unsettled by this but didn't try to persuade me not to meet Ravi. I spent the next couple of days in a quandary. After all those years of longing to be with Ravi, here he was apparently ready to make the commitment that I'd dreamed of. And despite the time we had spent apart in the past few months, I still felt the old familiar pull towards him, the ache of my love for him in my heart. But also now, I had tentatively begun to allow myself to become closer to Oliver, and although this was a very new relationship and not without its own difficulties due to his impending divorce, I could see that if a relationship were to develop between me and Oliver, it could probably be a wonderful relationship in which both of us were equally happy, committed and wholeheartedly invested.

The meeting with Ravi was very painful. He came to my home, and we sat on the edge of our seats as we talked. My heart was breaking, as I could see that Ravi was distraught. He pleaded with me and he cried. I had never seen him like that. He apologised for everything he had put me through. He told me that he understood why I had finished our relationship, but he was a changed man and things would be different from now on.

As I listened to him trying to persuade me to say yes to his proposal of marriage, the sadness in my heart was unbearable. I was hearing from him all the things I had wanted to hear for so many years. A part of me wanted to say yes to him. I still loved him. I was still so affected by being in his presence. I wanted to hold him and kiss him and take him to my bed. I allowed myself to try on the fantasy of this happy ever after romantic ending to see how it resonated within me. I was so tempted. But some wise part of my mind was speaking to me. This is the man who kept you at arm's length for so many long years. This is the man who couldn't accept the fact that you were a mother of two children who were not his, let alone love and support them. This is the man who watched you struggle as a single parent for years, trying to live two lives as a mother and a lover, never able to combine the two. And this is the man who created a child with you and then so coldly rejected this precious and miraculous gift and pressurised you into destroying it. And in ending the life of my unborn child, I had destroyed myself, abandoned myself so completely, and it had taken me years to even begin to recover.

As much as I was tempted by Ravi's physical presence, I listened to that wise voice within me. Although the relationship with Oliver was in its infancy, I knew that if I were to be with Oliver in the long term, I would be with a man who was brave and strong, a person I could trust. I knew that Oliver was a man with whom I could feel safe. The wise internal part of me also knew that, even if I did say yes to Ravi, judging by my previous experience, it was quite possible that he would backtrack and retreat once he had hooked me in again. I could not trust him.

So, I said no to Ravi. Softly, gently, but clearly, I declined to accept his desperate proposal.

The key thing is that I realised that it wouldn't really matter whether I said yes to Ravi and he withdrew, or I whether I continued seeing Oliver and it didn't work out, I knew in my heart that I was perfectly okay just as I was. I didn't need anyone to make me whole. I knew that I might have a relationship in the future or I might not, but either way I would be okay.

Ravi was devastated. It was a very difficult parting as I watched him walk away from me. His shoulders slumped. He was crying. Defeated and dejected. I stood at the door feeling my feet firmly rooted on the ground – strong and steadfast. I felt sad but I didn't feel guilty. I knew that Ravi had been hurt by my rejection of him, but I was able to cope with knowing that I had hurt him by acknowledging that my need to make him feel better had not led me to make a decision which did not meet my own needs. After Ravi had gone, I closed the door, I sat down and cried, but I knew I had done the right thing.

I received one letter from Ravi after that, his own version of ten sides of A4. It was the first time he had ever expressed his emotions in such an open and heartfelt way, in writing. In his letter, he told me how much he loved me, asking me again to marry him, pleading with me to say yes to him. It was a heart-breaking letter. I never did reply to it.

Afterword

Still

(The Commodores 1979)

It is now early 2022. The decision to terminate my pregnancy happened more than twenty years ago. You might be wondering why I chose to look back and share my story with you after so many years. You might imagine that the sensible thing to do would be to leave the pain of grief locked within a sealed compartment in the deep recesses of my mind – where it can no longer hurt me. In some ways this may be true.

I now have a very happy, abundantly full and settled life. Oliver and I are still together after fourteen years. We married in 2010 and we have a wonderful relationship in which there is mutual love, trust and respect. It's been many years since I last took antidepressants – I don't need them anymore. Thankfully, both Oliver and I now have very amicable relationships with our ex-spouses, and for this we are grateful. As for my long-held dream of going to India, I'm so happy to be able to tell you that a few years ago Oliver and I spent three weeks on a wonderful tour of Rajasthan, which was every bit as amazing as I had always imagined it would be. Although I haven't yet fulfilled my dream of doing some kind of voluntary work there, there is still time, and I plan to make this happen once the Covid 19 pandemic has resolved sufficiently to allow travel to take place safely. I'm hoping that Oliver might come with me.

It took a long time to gradually allow myself to be loved by Oliver, to even begin to feel safe and to trust. I often describe Oliver as being the least messed-up person I have ever known. He is happy in his own skin, open and honest about his feelings, generous in every way and completely unafraid to say a huge 'YES!' to life and all that it has to offer. By the time I met Oliver I was so accustomed to walking on eggshells, trying to second guess what Ravi might be thinking or feeling, trying to encourage him to live life to the full, instead of waiting for some perfect point of decisiveness, and trying to suppress my own feelings in order not to upset the precarious balance between us, that I found it hard to believe that it really was possible that I could be in a loving relationship with Oliver without any fear, on my part or his. Oliver is abundantly affectionate, constantly supportive and I still sometimes marvel at how easy love can be – much emotional healing has happened for me as a result of my relationship with him. At times, I am still caught by surprise with of a sense of pure amazement at the wonderful sensation of safety within a relationship – I really had no idea. I never take it for granted that I am able to express all of my feelings to Oliver, and he is able to express his to me, without judgement or censure from either of us.

I am eternally grateful that I am a mother. I realise that I am incredibly fortunate that fertility treatment worked for me and that I gave birth to two beautiful healthy babies all those years ago. I cannot imagine how my life would be without my son and daughter. As for my previous worries about whether, through my poor choices, I had given Evie and Daniel a bad role model for relationships, or caused them irreparable emotional damage from having a mother who was for many years immersed in repetitive cycles of depression and stress, I am relieved to be able to tell you that both of my children have turned out to be absolutely lovely young people. They are happy, kind and well-adjusted. We are very close, and they know that they are loved deeply by their mother. They both have successful, loving and contented long-term relationships with wonderful partners, and they are settled in their careers. One day soon they may encounter the challenges of parenthood for themselves – and I will make sure they know that they can always rely on my practical help and emotional support. They give me so many reasons to feel proud. So, to my huge relief, I imagine that somewhere along the line I must have got some things right as a parent. Sometime soon after I met Oliver, I remember Evie telling me that she would like to find a partner who treated her like Oliver treated me, with absolute love and respect, so I guess it wasn't too late after all for them to see what a good relationship actually looks like.

So, why am I dragging all of the past hurt out into the light now? The answer may be that I needed to be able to understand why I made the choices I made all those years ago, particularly the decision to end my pregnancy. In the cold light of retrospect, none of it made sense to me.

I have always been an avid reader, and admire anyone who can share their difficult stories with courageous authenticity. Risking disapproval yet sharing anyway. I have been helped in many ways by reading about other people's lives, yet when I tried to find anything which had been written about the lived experience of abortion, written from the individual women's perspectives, I could find very little which described the experience of a woman who had decided to terminate a much-wanted pregnancy, in the absence of any fetal abnormality, or in the absence of a severe health problem where a pregnancy could be physically harmful to the mother. You will have seen, having read my story, that this book is not a treatise on the rights or wrongs of abortion. I believe that all women should have the right to choose what is right for them. It is estimated that as many as 1 in 3 women may have had an abortion at some point in their reproductive lives – yet we do not speak of it. Research shows that the majority of these women do not regret their decision and often feel an enormous sense of relief. It may be surprising, but there will be a minority of women who, like me, are left with a profound sadness about the loss of their baby through abortion. I hope that if anyone who reads this book has experienced this unspoken and hidden grief, you might be helped by knowing that you are not alone.

Although I have gradually been able to create a happy and peaceful life for myself over the past few years, I can still at times be hit suddenly, as though with a sledgehammer, by a raw shock of grief when I think back to those times. My heart still aches with regret when I see something which reminds me about the abortion. I can be watching TV with Oliver, and if there is a scene showing childbirth, or a man reacting with joy when his female partner announces that she is pregnant, I will turn away from the screen and swallow my tears until the feeling passes. Sometimes even just seeing a pregnant woman or an Asian child will trigger a subtle and fleeting reaction. Oliver finds it difficult to understand at times how my reactions can be so raw after so many years have passed. It sometimes feels to me that underneath my apparently contented exterior there is a huge black hole inside me, which most of the time I'm not consciously aware of as I go about my life. Sometimes, however, when something triggers a memory of what happened, I can instantly be sucked straight back into that black hole where nothing exists other than despair and regret. I have tried for years to understand why I made the decision to terminate the pregnancy. To me, it was a planned and much wanted pregnancy. And it was a truly precious miracle that I had managed to conceive at all. I wanted that baby with every cell in my body. My motive for writing this memoir was to look back and try to understand why I made that choice.

I don't think of myself as being a weak person. I already knew that I could cope as a single parent. I know that I am resilient and able to cope with tough challenges. So why did I allow myself to become so utterly powerless that I allowed myself to be coerced into doing something that was ultimately so harmful to myself?

I could give you some 'reasons' such as those I outlined in my story. For example, my fear of how it might impact on Evie and Daniel if I had the baby, the uncertainty about how I would manage financially or practically with another child, without support, when I was just about managing with the two children I already had.

What I know now is that what really underpinned my decision was the fact that Ravi was not happy. He was angry. And I could not bear to see his anger. My fear of anger, and my need to put another's happiness before my own, cost me dearly.

I imagine that there may have been moments whilst you were reading my story that you wanted to grab me by both shoulders and shake me, to ask me what on earth I was doing in this ultimately destructive relationship with Ravi? Something that so many of my friends must have felt like doing as they saw me trying so hard, year after year, to make my relationship with Ravi work, when it was probably clear to everyone that I was chasing an impossible dream with this man. It was never clearer that Ravi was not capable of truly loving me than over what happened with the pregnancy.

I remember sometime in the early days after the termination, I kept trying to make some kind of sense of what had happened. In the midst of my blinding grief, I had a subtle awareness that maybe the soul of that little baby had come to me to allow me to learn an important lesson. I hold the belief that we are here in our physical bodies as humans on this earth to learn and develop as spiritual beings, and that everything which happens to us, all the people who come into our lives, whether good or bad, are here to teach us something. However, no matter from which angle I looked at the experience of the abortion, I couldn't identify even a single gift rising like a lotus flower through the mud of trauma – all I could see was an unbearable void of sadness. I do now finally understand the gifts that the baby brought to me. Being plunged into such a dark psychological place ultimately led me to seek help, and to learn how to create a loving adult relationship, to allow myself to be loved, and to learn how to truly forgive.

You might remember way back in the story when I began to suffer from frequent migraines? That episode marked the beginning of a long road of experiencing health problems, a myriad of unexplained medical symptoms. I have spent years traipsing from one doctor to the next, from homeopaths to various alternative therapy practitioners, trying to find the cause of my symptoms and seeking some relief from the constant physical pain and fatigue from which I suffer every day. Eventually, having been unsuccessful in my search for answers, and after being treated by many doctors as though my physical problems are probably all psychological, I began to wonder whether perhaps they were right after all?

A couple of years ago I decided to embark upon a year of weekly sessions with a psychotherapist to try to explore whether the roots of my physical pain really did lie in some deep and festering well of emotional pain which I carried within me. I wanted, and felt ready for, some really hardcore psychotherapy, a deep dive into understanding myself. I imagined that, possibly, if I explored the psychological aspects in this way, my physical pain and fatigue might disappear. When I started therapy, I felt like I had been rummaging around blindly for years in a huge sack, full of the jigsaw pieces of my life, and now the therapist had encouraged me to pour them all out onto the table, to pick each one up and look at it, and then decide how the pieces actually fitted together to form a coherent picture. At the end of the year of psychotherapy, although I was still in as much physical pain as when I started, I understood something about what the baby, and Ravi, had come to teach me. The psychotherapist helped me to start connecting the dots of my life experiences.

My friends and most people who know me would tell you that I am a nice person. I have made very few enemies in my sixty-one years of life. I go out of my way to please others and am known to be kind. I like to make people feel happy. I genuinely like to care for others. I enjoy being generous with my time and sharing the abundance in my life with others. These are all admirable qualities and I am happy to think of myself as a good and kind person. But this desire to please does have its downsides. I find it very difficult to say no to anyone, ever. No matter how much I might not really want to do something, or how it impacts on my own needs, I will often say yes to requests for help, or social invites, because I hate to think that I might cause disappointment for others. It can sometimes lead me to experience unexpressed and hidden feelings of resentment, of frustration that I have too much on my plate, or too many plates for me to be able to spin concurrently. My need to be thought of positively by others often outweighs any need not to abandon myself. I am terrified of rejection, and when I have experienced it, I find it very difficult to cope with. Psychotherapy helped me to learn that this behaviour is often linked to a lack of healthy personal boundaries – the result of a deep fear of rejection. As I get older, and with the help of therapy, I have become a little better at knowing where my own boundaries are and I am gradually learning to say no without fearing that the world will end.

I am uncomfortable with this aspect of myself, I perceive it as being inauthentic – saying yes to things when I might really want to say no – and I am striving to be more honest and open about my real thoughts. Perhaps writing this book and sharing with you some of my deepest failures is the ultimate risk-taking venture for me! I do fear what some readers might think about the decisions I made, particularly the decision to have an abortion, but the inexorable journey towards living my life as wholly authentically as I possibly can, in some part ameliorates my fear of rejection.

I have tendencies towards perfectionism, a terrible fear of making any kind of mistake, or of getting anything wrong, and although this in some ways helps me to achieve well in life, it can sometimes lead to me being over anxious about controlling the outcomes of a situation. Therapy has helped me to try to think as kindly towards myself as I do to others. I will always try to reassure another person if they are upset because they think they have made a mistake, but for some reason I will hold myself to a different standard and be comparatively hard on myself. As one counsellor once said to me "Who do you think you are that you should be so different from everyone else?!" It's a fair point, I think.

In my previous work as a nurse, I used to sometimes harbour resentment at colleagues who didn't seem to strive towards the same levels of getting things just right as I did, but I know that underneath my resentment is a feeling of envy that others can live their lives without having to deal with constant feelings of fear and anxiety like those that run through me like the writing in a stick of rock. My attention to detail, constantly tweaking systems and processes to improve patient safety, whilst a positive thing in some ways as it leads to a high level of patient care, is actually rooted in this mostly unconscious feeling of fear that something terrible is going to happen. I am always on high alert, looking for risks so that I can control outcomes. I am so anxious to please, so compelled to be liked by everyone and to avoid criticism or perceived rejection that quite ridiculously it can feel almost as though the world has ended if anyone is ever angry with me. I am so disturbed when a person looks at me with an unsmiling face or is cold towards me that I will start to feel panicky and will go over and above to try to make that person smile. My default internal reaction to an unsmiling face is to feel as though that the person must be angry with me and to assume that I must have done something wrong. I am mortified if ever I think I might have upset or offended anyone. This internal pressure makes for quite hard work and it is a totally unrealistic way for anyone to live. I have always known about this irrational sensitivity and panic that I experience when I see an unsmiling face but until recently, I could never understand this aspect of my personality. During psychotherapy, I learned about something called the 'still face' experiment. I watched a video which demonstrated this experiment. In the video, a mother holds her baby on her lap, face to face, and initially interacts with the baby by smiling and cooing in a very loving way. The baby looks happy and relaxed, and interacts responsively with the mother. After a few moments of this, the mother turns her face away from the baby and when she returns her gaze toward the baby, she doesn't smile or coo, but simply looks at the baby with a straight unsmiling face. The baby initially looks confused for a moment at this change in the mother's facial expression, but very quickly starts trying very hard to re-engage the mother so that the previous happy interaction returns. When the baby's efforts to do this are not rewarded because the mother continues not to smile, the baby then begins to grizzle, showing signs of emotional distress, panic and anxiety. After a while, when the baby's signals of distress still do not elicit a loving response from the mother, the baby becomes quiet and looks away from the mother. The baby gives up trying to connect.

Watching this video was a revelation to me. For the first time I was able to understand that my very earliest experiences as a new-born baby with my mother may have contained elements of the same type of interaction as I had seen on the 'still face' experiment. I can imagine that when I looked at my mother, I would have been seeing the outward manifestation of depression. She would not have spent much time smiling joyously at me. I don't blame my mother for this, rather I feel sad for us both. And I understand now, a little more, the roots of my deep fears about my own children feeling disconnected from me.

During psychotherapy, I began to understand how whenever I saw someone who didn't smile at me, my irrational panic was actually coming from somewhere deep inside my subconscious mind – I was still experiencing the same sense of fear and panic that the baby in the still face experiment experiences. Fortunately, now that I have a new awareness of the roots of my discomfort, when I do see someone who isn't smiling at me, even though I will still feel anxious for a moment, as these elements of personality will be hard-wired into my psyche, I am able to put a pause button on and remind myself that the other person's miserable facial expression is most probably nothing at all to do with me and is in all likelihood simply related to the fact that they might just be having a bad day! Whenever this happens now, I just have a little laugh at myself. I am reminded of an aphorism from the great author Maya Angelou, who said that all children need the kind of love that makes their parents' eyes light up whenever the child enters the room. I like the idea of this, it conjures up a sense of a child knowing that they bring unsurpassable joy to their parents, as though the child's very existence is a gift beyond measure.

Psychotherapy helped me to understand my personality by giving me a sense about the coping strategies I would have learned as a child in order to cope with my feelings of being overwhelmed, and being emotionally disconnected from my parents. Small children do not have the capacity to regulate their own emotions, and when they are feeling overwhelmed, they will rely on a loving adult to help them to feel calm and safe. When the child repeatedly doesn't receive this from the adult, the child is unable to manage her feelings, and so remains stuck in the feelings of being overwhelmed and fearful. The child eventually learns not to expect anything different from the adult, and develops unhealthy coping strategies to manage their anxiety, such as being cut off from their own emotions, or becoming a 'very good girl', not needing or demanding anything, always quietly well behaved. This can sow the seeds of becoming a compulsive people pleaser, as the child develops a mistaken belief that the individual's own needs are always less important than the needs of others. I think I can relate this to why I have always seemed to have a sense myself as being like an adult, even as a small child. I was a very independent little girl – in fact I was very surprised to learn that I even used to walk to school on my own as a five-year-old. I suppose it was probably normal in 1965, but when I imagine my own children at the age of five it seems unthinkable to me. As I was probably expected to just get on with things and not to expect support, maybe I never really learned as a child how to ask for it or receive it. I have always felt that I had an old head on young shoulders as a child. Funnily enough, I've just remembered that the very first record I ever bought was 'Lean on Me' by Bill Withers – I imagine that I must have related to the lyrics – wishing that I had someone to lean on.

So, what has all this got to do with my quest to understand what happened in my relationship with Ravi and what led me to make a decision to terminate a precious pregnancy all those years ago?

Ironically, although you might think that a person would choose a life partner with whom the relationship dynamic is very different to that of their parents in situations where the parent/child relationship has been difficult, anyone who has any understanding about the psychology of relationships will tell you that it is not uncommon for people to choose and become subconsciously attracted to people with whom they recreate the same problematic dynamics as those they experienced with their parents. Perhaps this might be because the patterns are familiar and fit with the template of that which we have been taught to expect as child. If you are interested in learning more about this, I can recommend a book called 'Women Who Love Too Much' by Robin Norwood. I clearly remember seeing myself on every page when I read it many years ago – I seemed to tick every box on the checklist for the type of woman who would gravitate towards, and remain in, a very dysfunctional relationship.

The psychotherapist believed that in my relationship with Ravi, I was perhaps in some ways repeating the dynamics between my mother and myself. I was trying to heal the wound of maternal disconnection by creating a different dynamic between Ravi and me, by healing the disconnection between us – almost as though 'this time I can make it different'. There was something about Ravi's emotional coolness towards me which would have felt subconsciously familiar. I did think that he loved me, just as I would have 'thought' that my mother loved me, even though I couldn't feel that love. With Ravi, I had to work hard to feel any evidence of that love. He didn't seem to be able to understand how I felt, or able to feel any empathy for my distress and vulnerability, particularly about the pregnancy, just as my own parents had not been empathetic towards me as a child. I had to suppress my own needs and not be too demanding. The more I attempted to draw the love and commitment I needed from Ravi, the more I expressed my need for connection, the further Ravi retreated from me. I wore myself out with trying to 'make' Ravi love me – to make myself loveable. I think now that one of the reasons why my intense sexual attraction to Ravi was so persistent and addictive is because I perceived his physical desire for me to be love, and indeed this might have been the only way that Ravi was able to express his love for me. It was when we were physically connected that I felt most connected to him.

So, to draw some conclusions to all of this navel gazing and psychobabble, I ask myself now whether I have any regrets. Do I regret that I allowed such a dysfunctional relationship to go on for so long? Sometimes, yes, I do regret that my constant emotional distress and distraction about Ravi will have impacted negatively on my ability to focus as a mother to Evie and Daniel. But I don't regret loving Ravi, or any of the beautiful moments that we did share together. I have a large collection of poems which I wrote for Ravi, especially in the early days of our relationship, which capture so clearly the joy I felt during so many of these precious times. I still feel genuine love for him. I don't regret having known that kind of incredibly intense love and attraction, even though it didn't work out for us in the end. I have sometimes wondered whether I did really love Ravi or whether in fact our relationship was based purely on a powerful sexual attraction. I can tell you that even now, when so many years have passed since my relationship with Ravi ended, I still think of him most days and can feel the pull of love in my heart towards him. I see reminders everywhere – in the clouds, in autumn leaves, in London, in certain scents. I have a box of mementos, tucked away in the back of my wardrobe.

Inside the box is that one hair which I couldn't brush from the bed, still wrapped up in a tissue. It is a reminder to me of how I much loved Ravi. Also in that box is the pregnancy test strip from the day I found out that I was pregnant with Ravi's baby. Those two pink stripes are the only physical evidence that the baby ever existed. Whoever has to clear the house when I die is going to be quite intrigued by the odd things I have kept in my collection of memorabilia!

Ravi and I are still very occasionally in telephone contact together, which Oliver knows about. When Ravi and I chat, we talk about our lives in general, family and work, but we don't revisit the difficult times. Ravi still lives alone and has never married, although I believe that he has had other short-lived relationships since we parted. He has no children. I don't like to think of him being alone and have tried to encourage him to find new love, as I know from my own experience that it is possible to love someone else without this in any way negating the love which Ravi and I shared. Ravi says that he thinks that relationships are too stressful to be worth pursuing – I wonder if perhaps his experience with me has put him off for life? It must have been difficult at times for him when I repeatedly ended our relationship – the way I used to reject him and then draw him in again would have been confusing and upsetting for him too. It was never him who called time on our relationship – always me.

I have a fear that one day something will happen to him,

perhaps an accident or serious illness, and nobody in his world would think to let me know. I might only find out a long time after the event. When Ravi and I were together, I asked him to carry a card with my contact details in his wallet, so that if anything happened someone would contact me. I don't expect he still has that card, so I just have to live with that anxiety.

I am extremely happy in my marriage to Oliver, I love him very deeply, but I think that I will also always feel love for Ravi in a corner of my heart. I will never know whether I may have been irresistibly tempted to say yes to Ravi's belated proposal of marriage if I hadn't met Oliver by then. I know that Ravi is a good person, but he too carries the wounds of his childhood, the impact of which is a fearful inability to make decisions or commitments. I also know that he would never have been prepared to do the exploratory psychological work required to understand his own psyche, which might have enabled him to participate fully in life. I believe now that my relationship with Ravi would most probably never have worked – I suspect that he would never have been able to immerse himself in my deeply committed love, in the warm waters of the oasis, or to give me the love that I needed. My friend, Lorna, once said to me whilst we discussing my relationship with Ravi, "Well, Jackie, you wouldn't go to a hardware shop to buy a loaf of bread." I had spent years repeatedly trying to buy bread at the hardware shop, and I ended up starving. Again, I am reminded of the wise words of Maya Angelou, who said "When someone shows you who they are, believe them." The clues were there all along – clearly visible there in the lines of the poem at the end of this book – a poem I wrote for Ravi in the early years of our relationship. The line which says that 'butterflies are not aquatic' is a clear statement about a fundamental incompatibility – I guess that I must have always known this on some level, but I didn't want to see it or accept it – so instead I chose to carry on hoping.

I will always regret my decision to terminate my pregnancy. Yes, even though I know that if I'd continued with the pregnancy my life would look very different to the life I have now, I do regret it, hugely. I believe that the long shadow of the abortion has been made darker in the context of my experience of infertility and an assisted conception. I think about the child that would have been here in the world, every single day. I wonder whether the baby was a boy or a girl, what my son or daughter would have looked like, what he or she might have contributed to the world. That baby was a person, just as I was once a fetus. I can't pretend to myself that this stark reality isn't true. I wish I could go back in time, and make a different decision. There are times when my heart physically aches with the pain of regret. In these moments I can feel such overwhelming grief that I almost don't want to be alive any more – I feel that I can't live with the weight of this sadness. I am remarkably unafraid of death, including the prospect of my own demise, and I wonder if perhaps some of this lack of fear of my own mortality might be rooted in a subconscious desire for life to be over so that I don't have to live with the sadness I carry. That's a pretty difficult thing to admit, or even understand. It's complicated – and not based in any lack of love I feel for those closest to me. I love my life, my family and my friends, and I'm definitely not suicidal, but these fleeting 'death wishes' do flash momentarily into my mind when I miss my footing and stumble through the hidden trapdoor beneath which my sadness lies. It is perhaps another subject to unpick if ever I end up having more psychotherapy!

I don't harbour un-forgiveness towards myself for the decision I made. Having written this memoir, I can understand now that by the time I was faced with that decision, I was absolutely ground down, and emotionally exhausted after so many years of unrelenting stress. It had been very hard work constantly managing Ravi's lack of enthusiasm for life. I had spent years in survival mode. I might be essentially a strong woman, but at that lowest point in my life I was completely drained of my strength and courage. I know that at the time, I was making that very difficult and time-pressured decision with all that I knew or was capable of in that moment. And I feel compassion for myself, not negative judgement, as I would feel for anyone else who had been in such a situation.

I find it interesting to reflect on the fact that although I have had a very varied nursing career with many changes of role, there has been a thread running through nearly all of these jobs, which is that of women's reproductive health and sexual health. I seem to have always been fascinated with the visual image of the pregnant female form, and am in possession of many artistic objects which reflect this. I have a collection of many goddess ornaments, one of which is a beautiful sculpture called 'The Source' by an artist called Philippa Bowers. This is a sculpture of a woman kneeling – she is around nine inches high. The woman has a hollowed-out abdomen, lined with sparkling amethyst gemstones. There is a space at the bottom of the sculpture where a tea-light candle can be placed. After the abortion, I used to light the candle and gaze at the sculpture, thinking that the hollow of her abdomen represented an empty womb, imagining that somehow, the light of the candle flames represented a flicker of life. On a recent trip to the town of Glastonbury, I was able to buy another version of 'The Source' which has a golden baby visible in the womb space. The two of them sit together, side by side, in my home, a reminder of two different parts of me.

I am interested in the idea of ancestral threads. How maybe we unknowingly play out in our lives some of the elements of our ancestors' experiences of trauma. I don't know much about either of my maternal grandparents, because my own parents didn't speak much about them, but I know that both of these women did suffer the loss of a child. I think it is interesting that both my mother and I experienced the loss of a child when we were totally unsupported by the fathers of those babies, albeit that the loss occurred for us in different ways. I do know that a thread of depression runs through the generations of my ancestors, particularly on my mother's side. My mother's hurt impacted on me, and my own hurt has impacted on my children. I hope that in my lifetime I have done enough to break some of the threads in order to break the cycle of pain.

I did meet with Ravi a couple of years ago, again with Oliver's knowledge, as I wanted to ask Ravi some questions to confirm the accuracy of my recollections about the timeline of our relationship in preparation for writing this book. It was a strange experience. Both of us showing the effects of the passage of time on our faces, we stumbled and faltered awkwardly in our conversation, but I could feel the currents of warmth and affection still there between us.

At one point, I asked Ravi whether he regretted the abortion.

"No...I do regret that the abortion caused the end of our relationship, but I don't regret the abortion itself...I don't really understand why you are still going on about it after twenty years," Ravi said.

"I don't understand why you can't understand it," I

replied.

"Well, it's just a procedure, isn't it? I anaesthetise women all the time for terminations of pregnancy. It's an every-day occurrence, isn't it?" Ravi said.

When I heard him describe my abortion as 'just a procedure', I experienced a sudden moment of clarity. It was like one of the moments when you see a clear image emerge as you stare cross-eyed at one of those magic eye pictures where, at first glance, all you can see is a complex yet meaningless colourful pattern. I was stunned by this evidence of Ravi's inability to feel any empathy for the distress I had experienced, not now and not then, all those years ago.

My eyes filled with tears as I looked at him and said:

"It was not just a procedure to me."

The Oasis and The Butterfly

I looked at your face this morning,
your eyes closed, keeping me outside the door
to your mind.
My heart ached, hurting with love and pain,
as I touched your body again.
I wondered how I will find a way
to let you go, as I know I must.
If I am an oasis, then I can't run away,
but if the rain stops falling, I become diminished.
No longer a lush and inviting sanctuary,
but a dry place with no purpose,
where nothing can grow.

If you are a butterfly, then you can take flight,
go wherever you need to be
at any given moment.
Perhaps I should take note of the fact
that butterflies are not aquatic.

I do not want to drown you
with the heavy water weight
of my needs.

(Written for Ravi on 14th January 1996 – two years into our relationship)